Fairy Tale Karma

A Novel By

D. Thrush

Book Bird

Cover and title page photos from Shutterstock
Drawings by D. Thrush
Author photo by David Peters

ASIN: B00M0THMPU
ISBN-10: 1500592587
ISBN-13: 978-1500592585

Praise for *Fairy Tale Karma!*

"Loved Fairy Tale Karma! *...I read this book in one day... couldn't put it down." Tavia*

"The last decent Cinderella adaptation I read was Ella Enchanted *by Gail Carson Levine, and that book was written in 1998! Here is the newsflash Ms. Thrush gives: you can't ever outgrow fairy tales!" Kelly Smith Reviews*

"Very funny read. Like a version of a twisted fairy tale. So clever... Gotta love the drunken fairy godmother who was banned from the castle! Hard to put down once I started reading." Autism Mom

"...filled with magic and imagination... I loved the twists and turns." Judy Hall Jacobson

"Surprisingly insightful: Not your average fluff tale... I liked this story but I wasn't ready for it to be so thought-provoking." BBomm

Novels by D. Thrush

Chick Lit

Fairy Tale Karma

The Daughter Claus (Book 1)
The Claus Cause (Book 2)
Merrily Ever After (Book 3)
The More the Merrier (Book 4)

~*~*~*~*~*~*~*~*~*~*~*~

Literary & Women's Fiction

Guardian of the Light

Whims & Vices (Book 1)
Fate & Flirtations (Book 2)

All the Little Secrets (Book 1)
Little Secrets Revealed (Book 2)

~*~*~*~*~*~*~*~*~*~*~*~

Contents

1 Happily Ever After?

Jill wondered if she'd made a mistake. Why had she worked so hard to convince her editor to let her go on this puff piece assignment? After all, she was an investigative journalist. What had possessed her to pursue such a trivial story? Yet something had nagged at her until she could no longer ignore it, though now it just seemed frivolous. Still, the Princess was expecting her, so she had to follow through. She was annoyed with herself and hoped her instincts hadn't failed her.

She'd driven a long way in her rental car to find the little hamlet tucked away in a hidden valley protected by rolling hills. Far from congested freeways, she passed through fields and dales, loops and hills aiming for what was over the horizon ahead.

Her goal was to do the interview quickly and return home to dash off the piece, exposing the Princess's fabrications. There was no such thing as happily ever after, and she intended to prove it, so that young girls would no longer fall prey to these silly fantasies and could get on with their lives. Once this was out of her system, she'd resume her career with more serious reporting. That was the plan.

Jill rounded the bend in the road that would lead into the center of the town of Quimby in the commonwealth territory of Wellstonia. What she saw made her pull over, and she rummaged in her oversized bag for her camera and opened the car door.

It was as if someone had painted this idyllic scene. A glistening white castle stood off to one side while the butter yellow sun illuminated the town in a warm golden glow. A vivid rainbow stretched across the sky as birds chirped in the verdant trees. A feeling of joy washed over her. It was as if her dreams had painted this perfect picture. She felt as if she'd stepped into a storybook.

~~~

Princess Ava glanced at the grandfather clock. She had her doubts about agreeing to this interview. What if this reporter discerned the truth? Not to mention, there was an unspoken rule of discretion among royals. The Prince would surely be displeased, but that wasn't her primary concern. Her attire was more important at the moment. She'd chosen a lovely cream-colored gown and a small tiara to greet her visitor. After all, she was a princess. How fun to dress up and impress someone from the outside.

Footsteps echoed from the hallway. The castle was vast and drafty, and the acoustics were terribly annoying. She stood and waited, striking a regal pose. Despite her tiny reservations, she was looking forward to sharing her famous story. It was a tremendous responsibility to set the bar for romance, and she took it seriously.

Sarah, one of the staff, entered with a young woman trailing her. The woman's hair was long and dark. She wore glasses and had a large fabric bag slung over her shoulder. She approached with an extended hand and quickly withdrew it with embarrassment.

"May I present Jill Graham, Princess," Sarah intoned.

"Your Highness, I'm not sure of the protocol." Jill appeared flustered.

Princess Ava smiled graciously and sat on a floral couch. "Don't worry about it. Have a seat. Just make yourself comfortable." She looked at Sarah. "We'll have some tea and pastries. Thank you."

Sarah nodded and exited.

"Thank you." Jill seated herself on a matching
~~~

couch opposite Princess Ava. "Please tell me if I do anything inappropriate. I'm not familiar with the protocol."

"Please don't worry about all that. I've never given an exclusive interview, so this is a first for both of us." She smiled to put Jill at ease.

"Okay." Jill seemed to relax a bit.

She studied the Princess, who was flawlessly beautiful with perfect smooth skin and silky, blonde hair. Jewels and gems dripped from her, and her necklace shimmered with a rainbow of colors, as did her earrings and matching bracelet. Rings adorned almost all her fingers.

"Why don't we begin with some background information?" Jill suggested.

"Such as?" Princess Ava asked. "Everyone already knows my story. Poor girl meets the Prince. We fall madly in love and live happily ever after. End of story." She leaned forward, and her soft blonde curls fell in her face. She brushed them back with a delicate hand. "I'm curious about why you contacted me for an interview. No one has ever asked for an interview before."

"Well, Princess, I want to know if that *is* the end of the story." Jill pulled a notepad and pen from her bag. "Girls of all ages all over the world want to know what it's like living with a prince. Can you really live happily ever after? I think there's more to the story."

Princess Ava looked toward one of the tall windows framed by long drapes. Sunlight streamed in, spilling onto the thick carpet.

"Has my story given people hope?"

"It depends," Jill answered.

Somewhere inside her was a shred of optimism that life could turn out happily ever after. She wanted so much to believe as she had when she was younger, but reality had callously squashed that dream under its heel.

Princess Ava's light blue eyes stared into Jill's dark brown ones. "Depends on what?"

"The truth," Jill stated simply.

Sarah entered carrying a silver tray that she set on the coffee table between them. Upon the tray were a small teapot and two white teacups with saucers. Flaky pastries and an assortment of cookies were arranged on a plate with two smaller plates beside it. She stood attentively.

"Thank you, Sarah." Princess Ava nodded at her and she quietly left.

Jill suddenly realized she was hungry after her long drive. She'd snacked in the car as she often did at her desk while she worked.

"Are you married?" Princess Ava asked as she reached for a cookie.

"Divorced." Jill placed a pastry on one of the smaller plates.

Princess Ava nodded and leaned back. "Now you're disillusioned."

"I think I'm more realistic."

Her mind raced with questions. There was so much to cover. She hoped to meet the Prince and tour the castle and the grounds. Then she remembered to get out her recorder. She pulled it from her bag.

"Do you mind, Princess?"

Princess Ava waved her hand. "Not at all."

Jill set the small device on the coffee table beside the tray and clicked it on as she took a bite of the pastry. It was divine, so light, it melted in her mouth.

Princess Ava smiled. "It's irresistible, isn't it? The best in the land."

"Yes, delicious." She delved in to the interview as soon as she finished chewing. "So, is the story true? Were you a poor, abused girl forced into manual labor by your stepmother until your fairy godmother helped you meet the Prince?"

"Absolutely. The gist of it is true. We were poor. I had few options in life." Princess Ave shook her head at the memory. "I used to look out my window at the castle and wonder what it'd be like to live in this beautiful palace."

Jill looked at the notepad on which she'd scribbled questions. "Tell me about your parents. Your bio says that your mother died and your father remarried. Your stepmother favored her own children and treated you like a servant. Is that true?" She gave the Princess a sympathetic look.

"I came home from school one day and my mother was gone," Princess Ava related. "I remember walking home from school. It was a beautiful day like today. There were some people standing on the steps of The Sleep Inn. They stopped talking and watched me as I walked by. I could tell something was wrong, so I ran the rest of the way home."

"That must've been difficult," Jill commented. "It's terrible for a girl to lose her mother."

"My mother was too young to wither away in this little town," Princess Ava intoned. "I mean to say, she was too young to die. She was pretty and smart and ambitious." She cleared her throat. "I mean, she could've done anything."

"Your father must've been devastated," Jill whispered.

"I think my father was in shock for a long time. We both felt lost without her."

"Understandably so. Didn't he remarry right away, so you'd have a mother?"

"Hazel ran The Sleep Inn. She'd lost her husband, and I guess she thought they could help each other," Princess Ava explained.

Jill reached for another pastry. She took a small bite. "Mmm. These are unbelievably good."

Princess Ava reached for one. "Aren't they? I have to be careful not to eat too many. The food here is so good." She poured two cups of tea. "Where was I?"

"You were telling me about your stepmother," Jill reminded her.

"Yes. I don't believe Hazel ever loved my father. I think she just wanted help with the inn. I had to do all the housekeeping. It was a lot of work, so much so, that I had to quit school." Princess Ava shook her head. "My father just never stood up to her. He spent most of his time at work."

"That's terrible," Jill responded. "What kind of work did your father do?"

"He was a bookkeeper. His major client was a dentist. That's why I have such nice teeth. He was always reminding me to floss." She opened her mouth to show off her teeth.

"You do have beautiful teeth," Jill agreed. "What else can you tell me about that difficult time?"

Princess Ava leaned forward. "That's when I realized I have a special gift," she confided. "Some people thought I was crazy, but that word is so subjective, isn't it? I'm just as sane as you are."

"I'm sure you are. And what is this gift?" Jill reached for her cup of tea.

"You have to understand something about this place. It's different. You can feel it in the air. Do you feel it?"

"Feel what?"

Princess Ava smiled and leaned back. "Magic. This place is enchanted. It's all around us. My gift isn't really that unusual in a place like this."

"Okay," Jill said slowly.

"The story is true. I can communicate with animals. The birds and other small animals were my friends and helped me get through the rough times until I met Agnes," Princess Ava asserted. "I know it sounds far-fetched, but remember where we are."

"Okay. So, the animals were your friends and

looked out for you. Now who is Agnes?"

"Agnes is my fairy godmother."

Jill grabbed her notepad and pen. Things were getting interesting.

"So, Agnes is the one who made it all happen. How did she appear to you?"

"I wish you could've seen her. She floated toward me in a sparkling bubble of light. She was the most beautiful thing I'd ever seen."

"Wow." Jill tried to imagine such an extraordinary sight.

"Agnes came along in my deepest moment of despair. She saw the grief and pain inside my heart. She knew what my destiny was and revealed it to me, and I cried with joy." Princess Ava dabbed at her eye with a napkin.

"How did she help you meet the Prince?" Jill asked. "Is it true that he took one look at you, fell instantly in love, and then searched all over for you?"

"Of course, it's all true," Princess Ava said.

Jill checked the recorder. "Go on. Then what happened?"

"Agnes saw my dreadful situation and vowed to help me. She knew that the Prince and I were meant to be together. She told me she would convince the King and Queen to host a royal ball to find a match for the Prince."

"And that's how you met."

"It was our one chance to fulfill our romantic destiny." Princess Ava sighed.

2 Animal Crackers

Ava ran home from school in a panic. Closing the front door quietly, she hurried upstairs to her room. She shoved her report card under her socks in a drawer and sat on the edge of the bed to catch her breath. She wasn't a good student. She spent too much time gazing out the window and daydreaming. Her fantasies were much more interesting than droning teachers.

She was tired of hearing her parents argue or, more accurately, hearing her mother yell at her father. Her mother was unhappy that she couldn't have all the finer things in life and that they were stuck living in this little town. Her poor father was a sweet man. He worked hard and had no idea how to please his wife. It was awful for everyone.

Ava endlessly dreamed of a better life. She wanted romance and adventure and everything that was out of reach. And her mother fed these lofty, elusive dreams.

"You're home." Her mother appeared in the doorway. "What's wrong? You look funny."

"Nothing. I hate school. It's a waste of time," Ava blurted.

"I know," her mother said soothingly. "You shouldn't be cooped up in this terrible place. The entire world is out there, but we're stuck here."

Ava turned and gazed out her window at the castle in the distance. It always made her feel better. It was like a shining beacon of hope.

"We can go to the royal gardens tomorrow," her mother offered. "They're only open to the public every other Thursday, and they'll be open from 10:00 till 2:00. We should go. That always cheers you up."

"I have school." Ava sighed.

"I'll write you a note. You can be sick tomorrow."

Ava loved the royal gardens, and strolling

through the vast expanse of walkways was her favorite thing to do with her mother. Flowers of all shapes and sizes blossomed amid the lush greenery and infused the air with fragrance. Magic glistened and lingered in the air. Ava could feel it. They'd stop and sit on a bench, and Ava would imagine that she lived there.

"Isn't the Prince my age?" she asked her mother.

"Unfortunately, the Prince will marry a princess. Those royals stick together like glue. The rest of us don't have a chance." Her mother scowled. "The only answer for us is to get the heck out of this town. I feel like I'm suffocating here."

"Mom." Ava wasn't sure what to say to her mother. "I wish you could be happy."

Her mother sat down on the bed beside her. "I made a lot of bad choices, and I'm paying for them. But you're lucky. Your entire life is ahead of you, and you can make the right decisions. Never settle. I want you to remember that. Never settle."

Ava never forgot her mother's words.

~~~

Not long after this conversation, Ava hurried home from school sensing that something was terribly wrong. She flung open the front door of their small, unkempt house.

"Mom!" She called out. She felt a chill at the hollowness of silence. This was not good.

She went from room to room looking for some sign of what was off and saw the usual clutter and disarray and dust on the furniture. She ran up the stairs into her parents' bedroom and flung open the closet. Her heart sank. All her mother's clothes were gone with the hangers in a tangled mess on the floor.

Ava sat dejectedly on the bed. She'd figured out months ago that her mother was having a fling with
~~~

Hazel's husband. She wondered if her father had known as well. Perhaps he'd confronted her, though she doubted it. He'd prefer to embrace denial.

Now she really felt all alone. Her father was a quiet man, and she could never recall having an actual conversation with him. She couldn't blame her mother. He was a boring wimp. They were too different. She couldn't imagine what had brought them together. It was a very sad day.

The town was buzzing with gossip. It made school even more unbearable. Her mother had run off with Hazel's husband, and everyone knew it. The rumor was they'd gone to Brazil. Ava sat in her room and cried. How could her mother have done this? How could she have left her behind?

For the last year, Ava had been attempting to befriend the popular girls at school and become a cheerleader. She wanted to be in the elite group at school. Maybe it would get her places. After all, it was all about who you knew and what you had. Her mother had emphasized this over and over, and Ava wanted to avoid the mistakes her mother had made and do things right. But now she was the subject of trash talk. It was so unfair to be the target of gossip because your mother screwed around, but that's what happens in these small towns.

Her father simply became part of the furniture. He wouldn't even go out except to go to work. Then one day Hazel marched up the steps and banged on their door. She wanted to join forces and do something about the situation.

Ava hid in her room. Hazel was a hateful, nasty woman. Her father feared her. Ava feared her. Everyone feared her. Ava couldn't blame her husband for leaving her. What did she think they could do about it, anyway? They couldn't go to Brazil and drag them both back.

Then the nightmare got worse. Hazel never left.

She took over, and Ava's father didn't know how to stop her. Her bitterness poisoned their lives. Fortunately, they couldn't marry because they couldn't get divorces from their wayward spouses. That was a relief.

Hazel had never had children, but she had two little yappy dogs named Elvis and Priscilla that enjoyed nipping at Ava whenever they got a chance. Their long nails clicked on the floor as they scooted underfoot, and they barked in their high-pitched squeaks at every little sound, sometimes for no reason at all. They snarled and drooled, and left mats of hair scattered all over the house. Ava never let them in her room and was glad they were restricted to the office at the inn since they growled at guests.

Hazel hated Ava and saw her as an annoyance until she realized she had a source of free labor for the inn. Then she took Ava out of school, so she could keep up with the housekeeping. Her father never stepped in to protest this decision. Sheer exhaustion consumed Ava, and she became even more lonely and depressed.

That's when she realized the birds perched outside in the trees and the mice that lived within the walls could communicate with her. Eventually, she found she could communicate with other animals as well. She finally had sympathetic friends who didn't judge her. It became her only joy in life. She would sneak bits of food to them and, in return, they agreed to watch out for her. They warned her whenever Hazel was approaching and reported the goings on at The Sleep Inn and in town.

One early morning, Hazel heard Ava talking to a bird about a cat loitering in the neighborhood. The birds and mice had been distracted by the lurking cat and failed to warn her.

"Who are you talking to?" Hazel burst into her

room and demanded.

"It's just Orville," Ava answered before thinking. She gasped and clamped her hand over her mouth. She hadn't meant to endanger Orville. He shook his head and flew off.

That evening Hazel screamed at her father. Ava crept as close as she could to hear his response. He had to stand up for her for once. Hazel finally had a reason to get rid of her. Her father listened as Hazel vehemently insisted on having her committed for her own good.

Ava shook with fright as Hazel's words struck her. If her father didn't protect her, who would? She'd have to run away into the woods surrounding the town and live on leaves and berries. She wondered if you could eat leaves. She certainly wouldn't kill any small animals. They were her only friends. They'd watch out for her in the forest. Perhaps they'd lead her to a cottage of dwarfs.

"That girl is crackers," Hazel exclaimed. "She could be dangerous for all we know."

"She's just grieving for her mother," her father mumbled in her defense.

"She's gone over the edge," Hazel hissed. "It's for her own safety. She's a danger to herself. And what about my guests? It will scare people away if they know we have a crazy girl working there."

"Ava isn't crazy," he said.

"You didn't see her like I did," Hazel insisted. "Her eyes were wild, and she was talking nonsense. I think she's dangerous. I'll call the doctor in the morning and make an appointment. I'm sure he'll agree that we can't allow her out in public."

"You mean after she finishes making breakfast and cleaning all the rooms at the inn?"

Hazel paced a moment. "Maybe we should give it some time. We don't want to do anything hasty. She needs the support of her family right now. Yes, that's the best thing for her."

"You're right," her father said meekly. But he had saved her.

Hazel stood with her hands on her hips. I'm glad we had this talk."

Ava scurried back to her room before Hazel could see her. She was safe for now. But she had to figure a way out of this situation. She looked out the window at the castle in the distance bathed enticingly in moonlight. It was so close, yet so far away.

3 Fairy Godmother Times Three

The first time Ava saw Agnes was late at night in the middle of town. She'd sneaked out and meandered through the streets, trying to get up the nerve to run away like her mother. She found herself in front of an enormous fountain in the park, staring at the stone angels pouring cascading water from jugs into the round pool below. A handful of change jingled in her pocket from tips, and she wished on each coin and threw them into the fountain.

She heard a ruckus behind her and turned to see Agnes stumble out of the bar across the street. They looked at each other for a moment. Agnes was older with gray, unkempt hair. Her clothes were rumpled and stained. She staggered past Ava toward the fountain, squinting into the water.

"How much do you think is in there?" Agnes muttered.

Ava looked down at the glinting coins scattered beneath the rippling water. Before she could answer, Agnes stepped into the fountain and waded around, scooping up the change.

"Hope there's enough here," she mumbled.

"What for?" Ava asked.

Agnes stopped and stared at her as if just noticing her. "I have to pay the bartender now, don't I? Don't just stand there. Help me."

Ava hesitated and then reluctantly leaned over and scooped some change out of the cold water.

"Really?" Agnes said. "You can do better than that."

"What about all the wishes people made?"

"Wishes smishes. Can't you help someone out of a jam?"

"Sorry. I don't feel comfortable doing this."

Agnes sighed heavily. "Fine. If you help me,

someday I promise to help you in return. Okay?"

Ava didn't believe her, of course, but she found herself shin high in the fountain collecting change. It was possible this old lady could help her someday, but she wasn't counting on it. Anyway, it distracted her from her problems for a bit.

~~~

The second time Ava saw Agnes was at the royal gardens. She went there whenever she could. It reminded her of happier times with her mother and served as an oasis of serenity. The myriad flowers soothed her, and the very air seemed to vibrate with magical possibility. She'd heard that there were sprites and fairies in parts of the gardens, but she'd never seen one. She had glimpsed peacocks a few times. They were skittish, but you could hear them. She was sure there must be other small creatures hiding amongst the flowers.

It turned out that Agnes had gotten a job as a guide. Ava tagged along with the tour. There were paths that meandered throughout the vast gardens, and it was interesting to hear about each plant and the history of the different sections. The queen especially loved the roses, and the bushes had been cultivated just for her. Mini waterfalls and large topiary animals were interspersed between the sections, and there was so much to see that Ava thought she'd never see all of it. She often fantasized about getting lost in the gardens and staying there forever. How lovely to be able to wander along the paths every day.

"Hey, kid. I know you." Agnes said to her as she filed out the exit with the others. "You look familiar."

Ava stopped and nodded. "I helped you at the fountain that night..."

"Say no more. I remember."
~~~

"You look like you're feeling better," Ava commented.

"Thanks, kid. I appreciate your discretion." Agnes grinned. "I owe you. Just let me know anytime you want a tour. I can take you into the areas where no one's allowed to go. I can show you the well."

"What well?"

There was the sudden sound of something shattering. It startled them, and Ava looked up to see a broken ceramic pot beside a bench. There was no one anywhere near it.

"Darn sprites," Agnes grumbled. "We lose more flower pots that way."

~~~

The third time Ava saw Agnes was at The Sleep Inn.

"Did you clean the room upstairs at the end of the hall?" Hazel demanded.

"There's a 'Do Not Disturb' hanger on the doorknob," Ava informed her.

"I've had a complaint from the guest next to that room. She said it sounds like they're wrecking the place," Hazel told her.

"Who's in that room?"

"Some crazy old hag. I should've never let her check in, but she paid in advance." Hazel tapped her fingernails on the front desk counter. "Go knock on the door and make up some excuse so you can look inside. I don't want any damage to the room."

"I don't want to do that. What if she's dangerous?" Ava protested.

"Just do it," Hazel said firmly and walked away.

Ava slowly walked up the stairs and down the hallway. She quietly put her ear to the door to see if she could hear anything.

"Who is it?" A woman's voice yelled suddenly.
~~~

Ava jumped. “Housekeeping,” she responded nervously.

The door opened a crack. “Can’t you read? The sign says ‘Do Not Disturb.’”

“I’m so sorry,” Ava stammered. “I just want to change the sheets...”

“Wait a minute,” the voice said. “I know you.” Agnes opened the door. Once again, she looked disheveled. “Are you stalking me?”

“It’s you,” Ava said with surprise. “I didn’t mean to disturb you. I didn’t know it was you. Uh. Can I get you anything?”

Agnes held open the door. “If you work here, then we both have problems. Come in, kid.”

Ava stepped inside the darkened room. She could tell it was a mess, even though she could hardly see. She carefully crossed the room to the drapes and pulled them open.

“That’s enough,” Agnes shielded her eyes.

“Are you okay?” Ava asked.

“Are you?” Agnes retorted.

And that’s when Ava melted down. She sat on the edge of the bed and cried and sobbed and babbled about her situation. She told Agnes everything because someone had finally asked, and she just had to get it out.

“And I thought I had problems,” Agnes said. “I’m just trying to get back on the wagon. I tell you that darned wagon is slippery.”

“I’m sorry I took up so much of your time.” Ava dabbed at her eyes with a tissue. “I must look awful.”

“Actually, it was pretty entertaining. I almost believe your sad story.”

“It’s all true,” Ava insisted. “I guess it doesn’t matter. I’m stuck. I’ll never meet the Prince and live in that beautiful castle.”

“What are you talking about?” Agnes asked. “Wait. I have to throw up. No. It passed.”

"Are you sick?"

"No. Just looking for that stupid wagon again. It's not easy. Is there a bar downstairs?"

"We don't have a bar. It's too expensive to get a liquor license."

"Good. I don't need to look for temptation. It will find me." She shook her head. "I'm like a homing pigeon. I go right for it."

"What?"

"You're not a good listener, are you? The bottle."

"What bottle?" Ava glanced around.

"The bar. Bottles in a bar. I'm like a homing... never mind."

Ava sat, collecting her thoughts. "I guess we both have things to overcome then."

"Did I hear you mention the Prince?" Agnes wondered.

"Yeah. It's always been my dream to meet the Prince and see the inside of the castle. I know it's ridiculous for somebody like me to think..."

"Hold on, kid. You're a pretty girl. Or you could be if we fixed you up."

"We?" Ava repeated.

Agnes beamed. "This is exactly what I need. A project. This is your lucky day."

"What do you mean?"

"Third time's a charm." Agnes quipped.

"What third time?"

"This is the third time we've run into each other. We've been brought together to help each other," Agnes explained. "I can get you into the castle, kid. I can get you a meeting with the Prince."

"Really?" Ava's eyes widened. "Do you know him?"

Agnes laughed. "This will be fun. Today is your lucky day because I am now your fairy godmother. What's your name?"

"Ava. I didn't know I had a fairy godmother. How

come I never heard of you before? Can you do magic? You don't look like a fairy godmother."

"I know I'm a bit of a mess right now," Agnes admitted. "Magic is complicated. It takes a lot of energy and focus. I can't use it for my own gain except for petty stuff, but I can use it to help someone. And it looks to me like you need some help."

"If you're my fairy godmother, then where have you been all this time?" Ava asked indignantly.

"We're around. We have to find our own projects. I know it's not very efficient, but that's the way it works." She frowned. "Okay, I know you want some proof. They always do. Go get me some clean sheets, and we'll come up with a plan."

Ava got up and went out into the hallway. Was this lady crazy? Could she really help her meet the Prince? Butterflies jumped in her stomach at the thought, but she shouldn't get her hopes up. Agnes was definitely off her rocker. Ava went into the big linen closet at the end of the hall and grabbed some sheets and pillow cases off the shelves.

Hazel accosted her in the hall. "Where have you been all this time?"

"Uh, I was talking to the crazy lady. I convinced her to let me clean up the room. There's no damage," she blurted.

"Good. Hurry up. We have other guests, you know."

Ava hurried back to the room. She often wondered why she was so afraid of Hazel. What could she really do to her? Perhaps she *could* have her committed. That'd be a bummer. Would she have to make the beds in an asylum? Maybe it wouldn't be that bad.

She knocked lightly on the door. "Housekeeping."

"Come in," Agnes called in a pleasant tone.

Ava entered the room and gasped. The drapes

were open, and the room was flooded with light. It was uncluttered, and the bed was neatly made. The room looked spotless. Agnes stood in the center, dressed in gray slacks and a black and white sweater. Her hair was neatly combed.

"Ta da!" she sang.

"How did you do that so fast?" Ava asked in disbelief. It would've taken her at least twenty minutes to clean up that room and make the bed.

"I used a little magic. It's not a big deal." Agnes waved her hand with a flourish. "Just put the sheets on the bed. I had to get you to leave the room."

Ava placed the folded sheets on the bed. "I can't believe this. It's amazing."

"I know," Agnes said. "I still got it."

"You never told me your name. I'm Ava.

"You can call me Agnes."

"Is that your real name?"

"What are you, the FBI? My real name is Anesianna Gisettaten Nuraletta Elysensia Sisinnalass. I go by Agnes. Who has time to say all that? You don't even want to know my last name."

"You're not from around here, are you?"

"Can't get anything by you. I told you, I'm a fairy godmother. We come from another place far, far away in another galaxy..." She chuckled. "I'm sorry. I couldn't say that with a straight face."

Ava furrowed her brow. "How can I trust you? I don't know when you're telling me the truth."

"Geez. Don't you have a sense of humor?" Agnes asked with irritation. "That long name is really my name. I come from another place, obviously, but that's not important."

"Okay," Ava said. "I have to get back to work or I'm going to get into trouble."

"With your stepmother? Do you want me to turn her into a toad?"

"Can you do that?" Ava asked hopefully.

"Probably, but I'd get in big trouble for that one. We'd better stick to the plan."

"We have a plan?"

"I think it's time to come up with one. This is the deal. The Prince can't seem to get his act together and meet a suitable princess. So that's where you come in."

"But I'm not a princess," Ava objected. "They'd never accept me into the castle."

"You're so negative. Let's see. You're young. You're pretty. You're... hmm. Let's use the word bright. You're a bright, pretty, young woman. We can do a lot with that. We have to figure out a way for you to meet the Prince. Let me think." She paced around the room.

"Can I come back later? I have to get back to work."

"Yeah. Yeah. I'll see you later," Agnes said distractedly.

~~~

Hazel came up to her after Ava had lugged some heavy bags up to a room and poked her. "That crazy lady wants dinner delivered to her room. Go see what she wants and then bring it to her. Make sure she pays you in advance."

Several hours had passed by now, and Ava gladly hurried back to the room. She was still finding it hard to believe that Agnes could help her. Was she just a crazy lady or was she really a fairy godmother? Ava was feeling a spark of hope, and she didn't want to be disappointed. Had she finally found a way out of a life of servitude?

She'd believed for a long time that her mother would come back for her or send her a plane ticket. But as each day went by, her hope had shrunk until it was a tiny bit of dust that disappeared under foot.
~~~

This small town had become her prison. She wanted so much to escape, but was intimidated by the big, wide world. It was a terrible dilemma.

"Housekeeping," she said as she knocked on the door.

"Come in."

Ava entered and was surprised to see that the room was, once again, dark and messy.

"What happened?" she blurted.

"Oh. It never lasts more than a few hours. That's the problem. I can't figure out that last step to make it permanent."

Agnes was again disheveled and plopped down on the unmade bed. She looked exhausted.

"What good is that?" Ava cried. "I was counting on you to help me. Can you do this or not?"

Agnes raised her eyebrows. "Wow. You really want this, don't you?"

"Isn't there an instruction manual you can read?"

"I'm not a blender. There's no manual."

"Well, what about a boss? Do you have a boss who can tell you how to make your spells last?"

"It's not like that."

"Is there a book of spells?"

"Geez. I'm not a witch."

"Then how did you learn all your tricks?"

"I'm not a magician, kid. I'm a fairy godmother. I was born into this." Agnes sighed. "It's too embarrassing to have to ask someone about this problem. Don't worry. I'll get better with practice. I just haven't done this in a while."

Ava shook her head in frustration and took a deep breath. "What do you want me to get you for dinner?"

"Run down to that sandwich place and get me the soup of the day and a grilled cheese sandwich on rye." She reached for her purse. "Get yourself something too."

~~~

Ava returned carrying a paper bag. She always chose paper over plastic. "That lady bought me dinner, so I'm taking my dinner break," she told Hazel, who was behind the front desk.

"What are you, friends now?" Hazel asked sarcastically.

"She's probably lonely. She bought me dinner, so I have to eat with her. I won't be long," she said over her shoulder as she hurried by.

"Being a shut-in sure builds an appetite," Agnes said, holding the door open for her.

Ava looked for some place to set the bag down. "You don't have to be so sloppy, you know."

Agnes swept some stuff off the little table by the window. "And you don't have to be so rude. Are you from New York or something?"

"I've never been to New York or anywhere else," Ava complained. "I'm not so convinced that you can help me, or even yourself for that matter."

"Excuse me for trying to get my act together," Agnes retorted testily. "Look, you little small-town loser, don't bite the hand that's feeding you."

"Hey! I've paid my dues, you fairy witch," Ava snapped.

"It's my sister who's the witch," Agnes said. "Don't get me started."

"Sorry, Agnes. I'm just tired." Ava smiled weakly. "Thanks for the soup and sandwich." Her stomach was growling.

"You're welcome."

Ava took a huge bite of her sandwich. She realized this crazy lady was the only one on her side. They ate in silence for a few minutes. Agnes studied Ava, and Ava dreamed about meeting the Prince.
~~~

"You have desperation and ambition. These are essential qualities for success," Agnes said. "We can do this. I think I got it figured out."

"What? A plan?" Ava asked hopefully.

"All we... *I* have to do is convince the King and Queen to throw a ball so the Prince can meet the woman of his dreams." She slurped her soup thoughtfully. "Are you legal?"

"Well..."

"That's okay. I think there's an exception for royals. They could probably marry a goat if they wanted. Anyway, they can invite all the single, young women in town. No, they can *proclaim* that every single, young woman must attend. They love proclaiming things." She nodded and smiled.

"But that's too much competition!" Ava griped. "There are cheerleaders who are prettier than me. Besides, I have nothing to wear, and I have no way to get there. There are too many holes in this plan."

"Don't worry," Agnes scoffed. "That's why you have me. I can take care of those holes and make you stand out so the Prince will notice you."

"But your spells don't last. What if reality kicks in too soon?" Ava whined.

"Geez. You're a negative Nelly." Agnes frowned. "You have to do some of the work, you know. You'll have to use your charm on him when you have the chance I'm going to finagle for you."

Ava looked at her blankly. She had a bit of mayo on her chin.

"Are you kidding me?" Agnes shook her head. "Okay, kid. We're in this together. I'll do my part, but you have to do yours. Let me get this set up before we worry about the rest. One step at a time."

Ava sat pensively.

"What?" Agnes asked. "What's wrong now?"

"I'm just wondering why you're doing this. What's in it for you?"

"Can't a fairy godmother do something nice..." She sighed. "Okay. It's good for me, too. I'll have someone on the inside."

4 The Prince's Dilemma

Princess Ava and Jill had moved outside. They sat on wrought iron benches in the royal gardens. It was warm with a slight breeze. The lush grounds surrounding them were endless. The birds chirped in the trees and bees buzzed. Princess Ava just hoped the garden sprites were scarce today. They could be quite mischievous.

"This is my favorite place," she told Jill. "It gets musty inside the castle. It's unavoidable because it's so old. I like to come out here and just sit and breathe in the fresh air and feel the sun on my skin. Sometimes I sit and read."

"You like to read?" Jill asked with surprise. "What do you read?"

"I like to read all kinds of things. Sometimes I read the classics, but I also like romance novels." She shrugged.

"But your story is the most romantic story of all," Jill pointed out. "Why would you want to read romance novels?"

"I just like happy endings." Princess Ava smiled. "Who doesn't?"

Jill nodded, but she was perplexed. She looked at the expansive foliage surrounding them. "Are the royal gardens open to the public?"

"They used to be but, unfortunately, people were trampling the plants and leaving litter everywhere, so I... we closed the gardens for now."

"That's too bad." Jill noticed a hummingbird flitting from flower to flower.

"The plants are very delicate," Princess Ava emphasized. "We have varieties of flowers and plants from all over the world, and we have a large greenhouse where we grow orchids and other plants that need more attention."

Jill nodded and looked at her notepad. "I'd like to

hear more about your fairy godmother and how you met the Prince."

"It's wonderfully romantic." Princess Ava sighed. "As I was saying, Agnes was a beautiful vision floating toward me in a sparkling bubble of light. She found me in a moment of deep despair. I was inconsolable after losing my mother, but she told me I was destined to marry the Prince."

"I want to ask you about that." Jill leaned forward. "I thought only a royal could marry a royal. Wouldn't the Prince have to abdicate to marry you?"

Princess Ava smiled patiently at the question. "Yes, in most cases, that's true. We were fortunate that the King and Queen valued the Prince's happiness over protocol."

"I see. That *is* fortunate. Please go on."

"Agnes went to the King and Queen and spoke to them about the Prince's dilemma. They wanted him to marry, but he wanted to be in love. He'd met every princess far and wide, and love had eluded him," Princess Ava related.

"So that's when they decided to have a ball and open it to the public?"

"Yes, they proclaimed that all the eligible young women were expected to attend. We each wore masks covering our eyes to remain anonymous." Princess Ava sighed again. "It was a perfect night. That was the night the Prince, and I fell in love. It was so powerful, we didn't notice anyone around us. He wanted me to take my mask off, but I was afraid that it would break the spell."

"Did Agnes use magic to make him fall in love with you?" Jill asked bluntly.

"Of course not. Magic wouldn't do that," she answered with indignation. "Agnes helped me with my gown, which was quite stunning. It was silvery white with a pale blue color that matched my eyes. I wish you could've seen it. She also did my hair. It was a sort of curly pile on top of my head with all these little ringlets framing my face."

"How else did she help you?"

"She helped me with transportation," Princess Ava answered.

"Anything else?"

"She helped the Prince notice me. You have to understand that there were so many young women who wanted to meet him and were trying to get his attention. He might not have seen me in that crowd. He felt obligated to mingle and try to dance with almost everyone, but they'd had a larger turnout than expected, probably because neighboring towns had heard about it." She frowned. "So, it was important that he notice me. Agnes helped with that, but magic can't make someone fall in love with you. That happened naturally."

"Fair enough," Jill responded. Then she heard a strange sound. "What is that?"

"It's a peacock. We have wild peacocks roaming around the gardens," Princess Ava answered. "You'll probably see one if we sit here long enough."

"I hope so." Jill glanced around and then back down at her notepad. "Tell me about the ball and the first time you met the Prince. I'm sure our readers would love to hear about what a royal ball is like."

"Of course. You never forget your first royal ball." Princess Ava smiled. "Every single, young woman was expected to attend. We all wore beautiful gowns and arrived by horse and carriage. Valets were standing by and escorted us into the castle. The ballroom was elegant and enormous. There were huge vases filled with flowers from the gardens. An orchestra was playing the most beautiful classical music. There were delicious hors d'oeuvres and expensive wines."

"Weren't most of the women too young to drink?" Jill asked.

"That's true. Some of us were too young, so they had special non-alcoholic wine," she answered quickly.

"Non-alcoholic wine?"

Princess Ava nodded. "I'm sure it wasn't real wine. Anyway, everything was the very best quality."

"Okay. Go on." Jill looked down at her notepad.

"Well, we all ate and mingled and waited for the Prince to show up. I think he must've been watching us from the balcony above. Once we'd finished eating and had settled down a bit, they announced him."

"Were the King and Queen there?" Jill asked.

"I didn't see them, but they may have been watching as well. A balcony with curtains encircled the ballroom. It would've been easy for them to observe us." Princess Ava explained.

"There must've been a lot of excitement when the Prince arrived."

"There was a hush when they announced the Prince. I think we were all holding our breaths in anticipation. After a few moments, he stood at the top of the staircase. He was dashing and handsome. He said a few words and then came down the staircase."

"What did he say?" Jill asked.

"He welcomed all of us. He encouraged us to enjoy ourselves. He told us to eat, drink, and dance. He said he hoped to dance with each of us," Princess Ava recalled. "He had this wonderful, full voice. He sounded gracious and humble. I immediately felt this powerful connection with him."

"It must've been difficult to meet him in that crowd," Jill said.

"Yes. There were so many of us milling around that I couldn't even see where he was half the time. Then I'd see him on the dance floor with somebody because people would give them lots of space. I kept trying to get closer to have a turn," Princess Ava said. "Somehow, we got closer and closer to each other. I could just feel something drawing us together."

"So then, you finally got your turn?"

"He was talking to someone, and he looked up. Our eyes met. It was like we were seeing inside each other and connecting on a deep level. It was a magical moment. I'll never forget it. He just walked right over to me. He took me in his arms, and we began to dance. We were in perfect sync and moved together as if we'd danced a thousand times before. It was the most extraordinary moment." Princess Ava dabbed at her eye with a monogrammed handkerchief.

"I can see how moving it was for you."

Princess Ava nodded. "We fell instantly in love right then. I can't even explain it. It just felt like it was meant to be. He didn't want to stop dancing with me, but he was obligated to dance with others. He made me promise not to leave. He'd go dance with a few women and then come back to me. He wanted to know all about me, but I didn't want to tell him anything. I was too embarrassed." She looked down at her hands in her lap.

"Did you think if he knew who you were that he might not be interested?" Jill asked.

"I thought his parents would think I was unsuitable. There were more successful families in town and he had his pick."

Jill nodded. "Did you tell him your name?"

Princess Ava shook her head. "My fairy godmother told me to leave by midnight, so I left when he was dancing with someone else. I went home and cried myself to sleep because I thought I'd never see him again.

5 The Health Nut

"Why haven't you gone to the castle yet?" Ava demanded.

Agnes was pacing in her room. "I'm afraid I'll blow it. I only have one chance to convince them. This is a long shot, you know."

"I knew I couldn't count on you," Ava said with disappointment. "Everyone always lets me down."

"Hey!" Agnes exclaimed. "You're putting a lot of pressure on me. I need to be in a relaxed frame of mind. I need to be loose." She shook her hands out. "Loose and relaxed."

"Maybe we need to figure out an angle," Ava mused. "What's in it for them? What do they want other than their son's happiness? That's important, but what would make them move on this?"

"That's easy. They need to continue the line. They want heirs," Agnes answered. "They want little royal grandbabies."

"There you go. Then what's the problem?" Ava asked. "It sounds like we have a good reason for them to have a ball for the Prince inviting commoners like me."

"We do, but..." Agnes looked uncomfortable. "We have a slight problem."

Ava scowled at her. "What kind of slight problem?"

"I kind of got banned from the castle."

"What?" Ava cried. "Are you kidding me? Our entire plan depends on you getting into the castle."

"Tell me about it."

"How bad is it? What did you do?" Ava put her hands on her hips.

"I don't really want to talk about it. I don't remember a lot, anyway."

"Oh, my gosh! You were drinking on the job, and you got fired. That's it, isn't it?"

"Hey, you're a good guesser." Agnes smiled brightly.

"Aren't you supposed to make amends to people?" Ava asked. "It's the perfect excuse to go see them."

"Unfortunately, it's a little worse than that. I thought it'd be funny to change the topiary animals into real animals." Agnes winced.

"That doesn't sound too bad."

"Imagine a dinosaur stomping around the gardens, especially with the sprites teasing it." Agnes shook her head. "It took me a while to figure out how to undo it, but at least nobody got hurt."

"So much for that plan." Ava stood by the window and stared outside, feeling defeated. "Is there anyone else we could send to the castle?"

"You. Why don't you go? You could deliver a basket of apples to the castle... Wait. That doesn't sound right. Let me think. We could have the Prince rescue you from a dragon. No, that's not a good idea. I'd better not conjure up a dragon. That could go terribly wrong. I could contact the Wizard of... No. He doesn't do outside jobs." Agnes sat down on the unmade bed. "I'm out of ideas."

Ava was staring at the castle in the distance. "I always see the castle no matter what window I look out of. Isn't that weird? What does that mean?"

"I don't know. It must be your destiny."

Ava whirled around. "You're right, Agnes. It is, and I'm not giving up."

"That's the spirit." Agnes stood up. "Now what?"

"This is what I want you to do," Ava asserted. "I want you to brush up on your magic, and then I want you to go to the castle. I want you to bring them a gift and apologize. Think of something they won't refuse. Then tell them about your brilliant idea for the Prince. Get yourself back in their good graces. Show them you've changed. You can do it."

"Maybe I should call my sponsor. She might be able to help. I need all the help I can get."

"Fine. Do whatever it takes. I have to get back to work." Ava went over to the door and put her hand on the knob. "We're going to do this one way or another, Agnes."

~~~

"Did that crazy lady check out?" Ava casually asked Hazel.

She hadn't seen Agnes for almost a week. Had she split? Maybe she'd gone back to wherever she'd come from. She wasn't really surprised. Agnes was a mess. What a waste of magical power.

"I certainly hope not." Hazel looked at the ledger book behind the front desk. "She still has a balance of $229." She picked up the calculator. "Then if you figure 15% for gratuities..."

"Gratuities? Why don't I get any of that? I'm the one cleaning the rooms." Ava reasoned. She didn't mention the tips she found in the rooms sometimes.

"Lower your voice," Hazel hissed. "The gratuities are for me for putting up with you. Now get back to work."

Ava trudged up the stairs. Someday things would change. Someday she'd escape this stifling little town as her mother had. Maybe she could find her mother. It was disappointing that she'd never heard from her. There must be a good reason. At any rate, she was going to create her own life just as she wanted it. It was going to be wonderful and exciting, and she was going to live happily ever after if it was the last thing she did.

She knocked on Agnes's door just as she did every day. "Housekeeping," she said wistfully. She turned to walk away, but then thought she heard something.
~~~

"Agnes?" she said into the crack in the door. She fumbled with her keys and opened it.

Agnes was standing with her back to the window. The room was flooded with light and was immaculate.

Ava closed the door. "Where have you been?"

Agnes was beaming. "I did it. I went to the castle."

"Why didn't you answer the door?" Ava asked.

"I just got back. I haven't been using the door. I've been avoiding that horrible lady at the front desk. She always asks me to pay my bill. Some people have no patience." She shook her head.

"The room looks nice," Ava observed.

"I've been working on my magic. The room has been like this since yesterday." She looked pleased with herself. "It could switch back at any time. I don't have a lot of control yet."

"What happened at the castle? Did the King and Queen agree to have a ball? Did you bring them something? Tell me everything." Ava sat anxiously perched on the edge of the neatly made bed.

"I told them two things that piqued their interest. First, I told them I knew of a business in town that wasn't paying taxes. This always gets their attention because they rely on taxes to run the castle," Agnes explained.

"What has this got to do with our plan?"

"I told them I suspected your stepmother hasn't been paying taxes for the inn."

"She hasn't?" Ava asked.

"I don't know, but the royal auditor will be a big headache for her for a while. It'll distract her enough to get her off your back and not notice what we're up to." Agnes smiled triumphantly.

"Perfect." Ava smiled in agreement. "What was the other thing?"

"I gave them hope. I gave them a dream. I told

them I'd figured out how they could have little grandchildren running around the castle in a year. Hope you're fertile, kid." She laughed.

"They let you in and forgave you just like that?" Ava asked with suspicion. "How did you get past the guards?"

"I had to bribe one of them. He's my sponsor's husband, but he didn't want to let me in because he's the one who got me the tour guide job, and you know how that turned out." Agnes rolled her eyes.

"What happened when you saw the King and Queen?"

"As soon as they saw me, they wanted to have me thrown out, but I told them I had a vision of little grandchildren scampering around the gardens, and the Queen perked right up. She loved it."

"Do fairy godmothers have visions?"

"I exaggerated a tiny bit." Agnes held her thumb and index finger close together.

"Did they agree to have the ball?" Ava asked anxiously.

"Well, first I said, 'Have I got a girl for the Prince,' but they didn't trust me."

"You really said that? Why? You could've blown the whole thing," Ava said impatiently.

Agnes shrugged. "It was a long shot, but it would've saved us a lot of time and effort. Now we just have to make you stand out amongst hundreds of other pretty, young women."

"Hundreds?" Ava repeated. "Do you really think that many will show up? This is a pretty small town."

"Trust me. They'll come from far and wide when they hear the Prince is looking for a wife. There's going to be a lot of competition. This won't be easy."

"What did I get myself into?" Ava moaned.

"You'd better start working on yourself," Agnes advised. "Watch your posture and everything you say and how you say it and always smile."

"How are you going to get the Prince to notice me? Can you really do that? Tell me the truth. I don't want to get my hopes up for nothing."

"Oh, I can do it. I just have to figure out the best spell. I'll work on that, and you work on yourself. Even if the Prince adores you, you'll still have to get the King and Queen to approve of you."

"Is that going to be a problem?" Ava wondered.

"Not if you keep reminding them about grandbabies. Hope your ovaries are ready." Agnes laughed as if this was funny.

"Stop saying that. I don't even want kids," Ava blurted.

Agnes looked horrified. "Never say that again. It's part of the deal. You have to give them little royal babies. Otherwise, they'll throw you right out of there. Don't worry about it. You can hire a nanny."

"Okay. Okay," Ava said to appease her. "I have to get back to work."

She was annoyed at this big concession she'd have to make. Why couldn't she ever do things on her own terms?

~~~

Ava was at the front desk when the auditor came in a few days later. She knew right away who he was because he was carrying a briefcase and looked very stern. He rang the bell even though she was right there.

Elvis and Priscilla began barking loudly from the office, and Hazel came out with irritation. He flashed a business card and asked to speak to her privately. Her expression changed to one of dread as she led him into her office.

Ava experienced a twinge of guilt and almost felt sorry for her. What if Hazel really hadn't paid the taxes? She'd be in deep trouble. What would happen
~~~

to the inn?

She could probably run the inn herself and do a better job. She could redecorate. She critically surveyed the lobby. As she was deciding on a color scheme, a young man entered and posted a notice on the bulletin board. It was odd that he hadn't even asked permission.

She went over to take it down, thinking it was some type of advertisement. But it wasn't. It was a notice about the royal ball. Butterflies leaped up in her stomach as she read the notice.

~~~~~~~~~~~

King Kellan IX and Queen Aurora
Proclaim a Royal Ball
In Honor of their Son
Prince Kellan X

All Eligible Young Ladies
Are Requested to Attend
Saturday, May 5
7:00 pm
Valet Service Provided
BYOM

~~~~~~~~~~~

It was really happening! Would their plan work or would her hopes be dashed forever? How were they going to pull this off? She needed a dress. She needed transportation. She needed to get a grip.

Ava picked up the phone and dialed Agnes's room. It rang and rang. She hung up and tried to hear what was going on in Hazel's office, but the voices were muffled. She was feeling very antsy.

Two of her mice friends scampered across the floor. She kept a bag of bread crumbs tucked in a corner of the front desk, and she tossed some on the floor by the baseboard. They stopped and nodded at her before gathering up all they could carry and scurrying away.

Agnes walked in the front door carrying a small bag. "Hey, kid. Do you want a bagel?" She held out the bag.

Ava shook her head and pointed to the bulletin board.

"Are you sure? They're still warm. What are you pointing at?" Agnes turned around and saw the notice. "Good. They're putting them up all over town."

"What's BYOM?" Ava asked.

"It means Bring Your Own Mask. It's a masked ball."

"I don't know about this," Ava said. "I have nothing to wear. I don't have a mask. I don't know how I'm going to get there. How is he going to notice me? This has to work." She felt terribly anxious. Agnes didn't seem like the most reliable person.

"Don't freak out. I've done this sort of thing before. So far, so good."

Ava leaned over the counter and said in a loud whisper, "The auditor's here."

Agnes looked over her shoulder at the closed office door. "It's all going according to plan," she said with satisfaction.

"Just tell me one thing," Ava beseeched. "I'll feel better if you tell me how he's going to notice me."

Agnes stared at her a moment. "Are you sure you don't want a bagel? No? Okay, more for me. What was your question? You know, you have to trust me. It won't happen if you don't believe."

"What do you mean?"

"You have to believe in magic for it to work. So, it's up to you. I've set it all up, and I'll do everything I can, but you're the one who has to make it happen," she explained patiently. "Don't worry so much. He'll find you irresistible."

Ava sighed with a bit of relief. "Thanks. I guess I just needed some reassurance. Nothing's ever gone right in my life. No one has ever really been there for me. I can't imagine this all working out."

"Well, start imagining it because your dreams are all possible. I don't want to waste my time and energy on somebody who's going to flake off. Do you know how much energy it takes to create magic? It takes a lot out of me. You have no idea."

"I appreciate everything, Agnes. I really do."

"Okay. I'm going up to my room to eat my bagel. Don't work too hard."

Ava was checking in a guest when the office door finally opened. The auditor brushed by her and went out the door. What had happened in that office? Was Hazel in trouble? She distractedly handed a key to the man wearing a baseball cap and sunglasses.

"Your room is to the left. Do you need help with your bags?" she asked him as she glanced toward the office.

"No, thanks. I just have one." He stood there looking down at the floor.

"Just call the front desk if you need anything," she advised.

"Thank you." He walked across the small lobby to the hallway.

Ava turned around and saw Hazel sitting at the desk with her head in her hands.

"Is everything okay?" she asked.

"We're being audited," Hazel answered.

"But everything's in order, isn't it?"

"Things are a little more complicated than that," Hazel said curtly.

"Are there problems?" Ava persisted.

"Mind your own business," Hazel snapped and slammed her office door.

The phone rang at the front desk, and Ava picked it up. "Front desk. Can I help you?"

"I want to order some food." It was their new guest.

"We don't have a kitchen," she told him. "But I'd be happy to run out and get you something. What would you like?"

"Oh. Thanks. I'd like a pizza."

"Okay. What kind of pizza?" she asked.

"I'd like veggies, no onions, with soy cheese."

"Soy cheese? I don't think they have that. I can ask, but I doubt it."

"I'm lactose intolerant. I can't have cheese."

"Well, I guess I can run to the health food store and buy soy cheese and bring it over there and see if they'll use it," she offered. "I know Gino. We order from them all the time. I'm sure they'll do it."

"Very good. Thank you." He hung up the phone abruptly.

"Hazel." She knocked on the door to the office, and the dogs started barking. "I have to go out and get some food for a guest."

"Hurry up," Hazel called back from behind the door.

Ava shook her head. She seemed to be at the beck and call of everyone. She was a little angry at herself. Sometimes she was too nice. After all, what did anyone ever do for her? But her exasperation dissipated in the fresh air and sunlight. It felt good to be outside. The air was cool, but the sun was warm on her skin.

Three squirrels chased each other in the trees, jumping nimbly from branch to branch. One of them stopped briefly and raised a paw to wave at her. She smiled and waved back. And then they were gone.

She looked longingly at the castle. It'd be so nice to have people waiting on her for a change. But who was she kidding? Even if the Prince noticed her, the

King and Queen would never let him marry her. Marrying a commoner was one thing, but marrying a maid was surely something they would never accept.

Ava ran over to The Health Nut, which was a little health food store a few blocks over. She hoped they'd have soy cheese. She'd never been inside but had heard that they carried organic produce, vitamins, and other specialized items.

It was a funky little store. She strolled down the aisles to see what kinds of food items they carried. There was a variety of organic canned and packaged products and a colorful display of organic produce. There were vitamins and supplements. She'd never heard of many of these things. She came upon the refrigerated section. It held many more things she'd never heard of. There were non-dairy cheeses made from soy and almonds and rice. Who knew these things existed? She chose some soy cheese and waited at the register. There was an enticing display of organic, dark chocolate bars. She impulsively picked one up and set it next to the soy cheese.

Darn! She'd forgotten Hazel's credit card. Luckily, she had cash on her from the tips she'd hidden in her pockets.

Then she hurried over to the pizza place. Thankfully, this was a small town, and she could get everywhere on foot. Gino agreed to use the soy cheese and told her they'd deliver it in a half hour. Guaranteed.

Hazel was behind the front desk when she got back. "What took you?" she demanded. "Go upstairs. That crazy lady wants something."

Ava stashed the chocolate bar in the cleaning closet and went upstairs. She knocked on Agnes's door. "It's me," she said.

"Come in," Agnes called out.

Ava opened the door, not knowing what to expect. The room was tidy. She walked in and sat on the cushioned chair by the window. Agnes was sitting on the edge of the bed.

"Have you ever heard of soy cheese?" Ava asked her.

"Yeah. They have it at The Health Nut. Why?" Agnes furrowed her brow. "It's interesting that you'd ask me that."

"Why? Are you lactose intolerant, too?"

"I'm actually gluten intolerant. Are you lactose intolerant?" Agnes asked.

"No, it's just a guest. How can you be gluten intolerant? I saw you eating a bagel."

"Yeah, I'm actually sensitive to gluten and I'm not supposed to eat it, but I couldn't help myself. Do they have gluten-free bagels at The Health Nut?" she asked hopefully.

"I don't know," Ava answered impatiently. "Did you tell Hazel you wanted to see me? I don't have much time. She keeps tabs on me."

"Yeah. I wanted to talk to you about your gown. We have to plan your outfit. Then there are the shoes and your hair. There's so much to do."

Ava sighed. "I don't have any money for a gown or shoes. I don't even know if I should bother. I must be crazy to think that the Prince will even notice me."

"Hey, have you forgotten who I am?" Agnes demanded. "I'm your fairy godmother. We don't need money. I'm going to create the perfect gown for you. You're going to look fabulous. The Prince will be smitten you. I'll make sure of it."

"But even if he does, they'll never let him marry a maid," Ava whined. "It'll never happen. Nothing ever works out."

"Geez." Agnes rolled her eyes. "Do you know how lucky you are to have this opportunity with me on your side? It wasn't easy to set this up. I won't let you blow it with your attitude."

"I just don't know." Ava was afraid to get her

hopes up. Her mother had told her to never settle, but Hazel had beaten down her dreams.

"You don't know how much I want to turn you into a gnat right now," Agnes exclaimed suddenly.

"Go ahead!" Ava cried. "I'd be better off."

"Wow." Agnes took a deep breath. "It must suck to be you."

Ava looked out the window at the castle. She was filled with longing for a better life. "I wish..."

"Yes," Agnes encouraged. "I want you to wish. I want you to believe. We're in this together. Trust me and believe in magic."

"I belong in that castle," Ava affirmed.

"I'm thinking a soft off-white gown with blue to match your eyes," Agnes studied her.

"I'm hungry." She thought of the chocolate bar in the closet. "I have to get back to work."

"Come back tomorrow," Agnes ordered. "I'll work on the gown tonight."

Ava could smell the pizza as she came down the stairs. She snagged the chocolate bar out of the closet.

"There you are," Hazel said. "Do you know who ordered this pizza?"

"It's for the new guest I checked in. I'll take it."

"I'll add it to his bill." Hazel went back into the office.

Ava knocked on his door. Now she was delivering pizza. What next?

He opened the door a crack. He still had on his baseball cap and sunglasses. He saw the pizza and opened the door wide to let her in. His unopened suitcase was on the bed. The TV was on with the sound turned down. The drapes were half open.

She set the pizza on the little table by the window. "There you go. We'll bill it to your room."

He opened the box. "This looks good. Did they use soy cheese?"

"Yes. I went to the health food store and bought it myself. Did you know they also have almond cheese and rice cheese?" she asked.

"I didn't know that," he answered. "I'll have to try them."

Ava's stomach rumbled loudly. She smiled with embarrassment.

"Have you ever had soy cheese?" he asked as he sat down. "Why don't you try it? I can't eat all this."

"Thanks." She gratefully pulled out a chair and sat opposite him. The pizza smelled delicious, and she was starving. Before she knew it, she was on her second slice. She didn't care what kind of weird cheese was on it. It tasted fine to her and satisfied her growling stomach.

He took off his sunglasses, and she noticed his dark eyelashes and eyebrows. His hair curled out from under his cap. She wondered where he was from and where he was going. She often wondered about guests. She wished she could travel as freely.

"I've always wanted to travel," she said, glancing at the TV.

A commercial depicted a sunny, tropical beach with swaying palm trees and aqua blue water. She wondered if Brazil was like that and if she'd see it someday.

He looked at the TV. "I wouldn't mind being there right now." He smiled. "I'd like to lie on a beach with not a care in the world. Nobody would bother me, and I could stare at the ocean for hours or read a book or take a nap."

"That sounds nice," she agreed. "Do you think Brazil's like that?"

"Brazil is warm and tropical. It has an enormous coastline and beautiful rainforests. It's so important to protect the rainforests." He shook his head with a slight frown. Then he smiled and leaned forward. "But what I'd like is to have my own island and escape from everyone."

"That sure would be nice," she said. "But there wouldn't be any stores for food and supplies."

"Well, you just figure out how to capture and filter rainwater and build a shelter and eat a lot of fruit." He laughed.

She laughed too. "What? No pizza?"

"I guess there are things I'd miss," he confessed.

"I sure wouldn't mind running away to a tropical paradise."

"This probably isn't your ideal job," he acknowledged. "Do you work here every day after school?"

"My stepmother took me out of school, so I could work here all the time," she said sadly.

"That's awful," he sympathized.

"I have plans to get out of here," she told him so she wouldn't sound like a complete loser. She glanced out the window at the castle. "What about you? Are you on your way somewhere?"

"I'm kind of like you. I'm stuck, and I'm trying to get unstuck." His eyes drew hers. "It seems like everyone else has always made all my decisions for me. It's like I've never really had any choices."

"Exactly." She remembered the chocolate bar in her pocket. "Hey, I have dessert." She set it on the table between them.

"Organic, dark chocolate? I love dark chocolate."

He grinned at her, and some little spark within her dispelled all her doubts and fears. She looked over at the clock on the bedside table.

"Do you have to go?" he asked with disappointment.

"I should go," she admitted. "I have work to do."

He pushed the chocolate bar toward her. "Save this for next time. Come back when you have a break, and we'll share it then."

"Okay," she agreed happily.

Ava left his room and went straight to the cleaning supply closet to stash the chocolate bar before she went back to the front desk.

"What took you?" Hazel demanded. "Stop getting all chummy with the guests."

"I had some pizza. That was my lunch," Ava answered defensively.

"Fine. I need you to take the dogs for a walk. I'll get their leashes." She opened the office door, and Ava could hear Elvis and Priscilla yapping.

She realized she didn't even know the new guest's name. She pulled out the registration book to find it and quickly ran her finger down the names. There it was. Kent Clark. Kent was his name. Kent...

"Come on, sweeties," Hazel coaxed as she came out of the office with the dogs. Their nails clicked and slipped on the floor as they pulled on their leashes. "Here." She handed them to Ava. "Make sure they go before you bring them back."

6 Royal In-Laws

The sun had moved, and the benches were draped in shade. Sarah had brought out sandwiches and lemonade for Princess Ava and Jill. Princess Ava had dropped pieces of her sandwich behind the bench for the sprites when Jill wasn't looking. Hopefully, it would appease them and they'd behave.

Jill was concentrating on reviewing her notes when she heard something and looked up.

A small, older woman with a gilded cane tottered toward them. She wore a long, royal blue dress and a matching hat with a short veil covering her face.

"Kell," she called. "Where is that boy?"

Princess Ava's composure immediately dissolved. She jumped up from the bench, almost spilling her lemonade.

"Mother! What are you doing out here?"

The woman was slightly bent over, and she looked up at Princess Ava. "I'm not your mother," she said testily. "I'm looking for Kell. He always hides in the gardens. Where is that boy?"

"I think he's inside," Princess Ava said, attempting to divert her.

"I don't have time for a ride," the woman said impatiently. "Who are you?"

"Why don't you look inside? I think Kell is inside." Princess Ava tried to direct her back towards the castle.

"I know it's cold inside. I'm just going to sit out here for a while. It's quite warm for winter. Where are the holiday decorations?" She slowly made her way to a bench, tapping her cane on the cobblestone path.

Jill looked at Princess Ava, waiting for an introduction. She had an idea who this might be, and she was thrilled to have this opportunity.

The woman settled herself on a bench. "Who are

you?" She glared at Jill.

Princess Ava sat down beside her. "This is Jill. She's interviewing me for an article about the royal family." She sighed and looked at Jill. "This is my mother-in-law, Queen Aurora. You should stand and curtsy."

Jill jumped up. Her notepad and pen fell off her lap. She did her best to curtsy. "Your Highness, I'm so happy to meet you."

"I don't have time for a reception line," Queen Aurora mumbled.

"The gardens are lovely." Jill sat back down and picked up her pen and notepad.

"Mother, have you had anything to eat?" Princess Ava asked.

"No, I don't mind the heat." The Queen fanned herself. "Where are all the children? They love running around the gardens. Where's the nanny?"

"They all went home," Princess Ava answered.

"No, I don't want to be alone. You can stay if you don't scare off the children," Queen Aurora said. "Have you seen the Prince? He loves to play hide and seek in the gardens." She smiled at the memory. "But now I can't seem to find him."

"He is a good hider," Princess Ava agreed.

"What did you say?" The Queen looked at her with a puzzled expression.

"I said he hides very well."

"Who are you talking about?" Queen Aurora asked. "You're not making any sense."

Princess Ava shook her head in frustration. Then she spotted Sarah on the path to the castle. "She's over here, Sarah," she called.

Sarah rushed over. "I'm so sorry, Princess. She wandered off when I wasn't looking. I'll get her back inside."

"Why don't you take her for a little walk first? It'll be good for her," Princess Ava suggested.

"Your Highness, let's go see how the roses are doing." Sarah helped the Queen to her feet.

"I love the roses," the Queen said as she toddled off with Sarah.

"So that's Queen Aurora," Jill said, watching them.

"Yes." Princess Ava sighed. "I'm sure you can see she has memory issues, and she's hard of hearing."

"That must be difficult for everyone," Jill commented. "I think our readers will relate. There are a lot of adults dealing with parents with dementia."

"Oh, please don't put that in your article. I know my husband would rather deal with this privately," Princess Ava implored.

"There's nothing to be embarrassed about, Princess. So many people are dealing with this. I think it's good to know that wealth doesn't insulate you from life. I think our readers will sympathize, and it will make you more relatable..."

"Please," Princess Ava repeated. "It's not my decision to make. They're my husband's parents, and it's up to him, and I know how he feels about it."

"Okay. I'll put it on hold for now," Jill relented.

"I appreciate it. I feel comfortable sharing, but my husband is used to discretion."

He was very touchy about their privacy. He wasn't supportive of this interview, but Princess Ava had seen it as an opportunity to reinforce their love story. Okay, so her version was a little embellished, but it was essential to preserve the fantasy of their charmed life. She was living the dream to which young girls could aspire.

"And that's why this interview is so important," Jill was saying. "Our readers need to see that you're real people with actual problems, just like everyone else."

"I don't need any help," an older man spat out at

a young woman who helping him navigate the cobblestone path.

Princess Ava groaned. “Here comes my father-in-law. They seem to get restless at this time of day.” She got up and went over to him.

Jill stood up and watched. She couldn’t believe her luck in getting to see the Queen and King in one day.

“Father Kellan, may I help you?”

Princess Ava took his arm and led him towards the bench. He leaned on his intricately carved wooden cane and hobbled along.

The female staff member trailed behind them. “I’m sorry, Princess. He insisted on coming outside.”

“That’s okay, Susan. Queen Aurora is out here too.”

The three of them sat down on the bench.

Jill curtsied awkwardly. “Your Highness. It’s an honor.”

He waved his hand dismissively, and she sat back down on the bench opposite them.

He turned to Princess Ava. “Where’s Rory?”

“She’s taking a walk in the gardens,” she told him. “It’s a beautiful day.”

He looked at Jill with suspicion. “Who’s this?”

“This is Jill. She’s interviewing me for an article. People want to know about us,” she explained.

“What do they want to know?” he grumbled.

“People would like to know what it’s like to live in this beautiful castle and be a part of the royal family.” Jill leaned forward, eager to take this chance to talk to the King. “Can I ask you some questions? How did you meet Queen Aurora?”

King Kellan scowled and looked at Princess Ava. “What did she say?”

“She wants to know how you met Queen Aurora,” she said loudly.

“I don’t know where she is,” he sputtered

impatiently. He looked back at the castle. "This place is too big."

Princess Ava looked at Susan. "Why don't you take him for a walk in the gardens? Sarah was taking the Queen over to the roses. Maybe you can catch up with them."

Susan nodded and jumped up. "Your Highness, the Queen is waiting for you by the roses."

His face softened. "She loves the roses."

She helped him up, and they continued along the path through the flowers and greenery. His cane clacked on the cobblestones.

"I'm glad I got to meet the King and Queen," Jill said. "In their day they were a striking couple."

Princess Ava turned her gaze to Jill. "Nowadays they spend most of their time looking for each other."

7 Chocolate Kiss

Ava had gone to the post office for Hazel and was on her way back when she heard Orville. She always recognized his unique chirp. She hadn't seen him for a while and listened while he relayed an important message to her.

"Really?" She looked up into the tree. She listened as he chirped more news. She furrowed her brow for a moment. "I'll go tell Agnes. Maybe she knows something. Thanks, Orville."

He'd imparted some interesting information. She raced back to the inn, hoping she could zip up to Agnes's room before Hazel asked her to do something else.

Hazel was in her office on the phone, so Ava ran up the stairs and knocked urgently on Agnes's door. "It's me," she said to the door. "Let me in."

"Enter," Agnes called cheerfully.

Ava burst through the door and quickly closed it behind her. The first thing she saw was a stunning gown on a headless mannequin in the middle of the room. It was ice blue and pale cream. It took her breath away.

"I knew you'd like it," Agnes blurted, barely able to contain herself. "Try it on. I can't wait to see it on you."

"How did you do this? Did you make this with magic?"

"Oh, a little of this, a little of that. Come on. Try it on," Agnes encouraged.

Ava quickly shed her shirt and pants, and Agnes helped her carefully pull the gown over her head. Ava stood in her socks while Agnes fastened and zipped and snapped it onto her until it snugly hugged her body. Ava wasn't used to form-fitting outfits. She usually wore loose clothing in which to work.

"I wish we had a full-length mirror so I could see

myself," Ava said.

"Turn around," Agnes told her.

Ava slowly turned, feeling the gown swish around her. She looked up to see a full-length oval mirror on a stand. She gasped at the sight of herself.

"It fits perfectly. It's gorgeous. Oh, my gosh, Agnes. It's beautiful. Thank you so much." She couldn't believe how stunning she looked.

"Don't you love it?" Agnes asked with excitement. "I knew you would." She stood behind Ava and lifted her hair. "We'll sweep your hair up like this and have some little curls around your face. What do you think?"

"Whatever you think. You're good at this."

"I know." Agnes sighed. "I forgot how fun it is."

"I almost forgot!" Ava said suddenly. "Orville told me they might cancel the ball."

"What? No way!" Agnes cried. "Who's this Orville, and how would he know this?"

"He was hanging out over by the castle, and he overheard some things. All he knows is that there's something going on, and it's a big problem."

"I can't believe my sources didn't tell me about this. Maybe the Prince doesn't want to go through with it. I don't think he's gung-ho about being set up and forced into marriage."

"He doesn't want to get married?" Ava asked, crestfallen.

"Don't worry," Agnes assured her. "No one wants to get married until they think they meet the One. Something else must be going on. I'll find out. See if your friend Orwell can find out more. Who is he, anyway?"

"Orville is a bird. I trust him."

"Ah, an avian informer. Good. Maybe he can find out more. Keep me posted. Now let's get that dress off before it wrinkles. I think I'll play around with the colors. Silver might work better."

~~~

Ava knocked on Kent's door. "I brought chocolate," she called in to him.

He opened the door with a big smile. "You're back. I thought you ate it all by yourself." He had on his usual baseball cap.

"I wouldn't do that." She stepped into the room and closed the door behind her. "Hazel has been keeping me pretty busy."

They sat at the table by the window. Ava ripped open the wrapper and broke the bar into squares. They each popped a piece into their mouths.

He picked up the wrapper and looked at it. "Organic. Fair trade. No refined sugar. Excellent choice."

"Mmm." She let the chocolate melt in her mouth. It was rich and tasted delicious. That's all she cared about.

"You never told me your name," he said.

"Ava," she answered. "I saw your name on the register. Kent."

"Ava."

She smiled at the sound of his voice saying her name.

"So, Ava," he said, placing another square of chocolate into his mouth. He held one before her lips, and she opened her mouth. "What's a nice girl like you doing in a place like this?"

They both laughed.

"I don't know. I just work here," she said, and they laughed again.

"Seriously," Kent said. "What are your plans? What do you want to do with your life?"

A vision of the castle floated in her head. She couldn't tell him that her dream was simply to live in the castle. It sounded so unimaginative.
~~~

She shrugged. "I just want to get out of here. What about you?"

"Me, too. I think our plans need to be a little more specific." He grinned at her.

Ava contemplated this for a moment. What *did* she want besides a life of luxury in the castle? What drew her? What did she really want?

"I guess I just want to go where I want and have what I want and not have anybody ordering me around," she surmised.

"That sounds good." Kent nodded. "I think it'd be fun to travel on the spur of the moment. You know? Go anywhere and take whatever road looks appealing and not have anyone expect anything of you."

"What's stopping you?" she wondered. "You're old enough to do whatever you want. You can go anywhere. I'm not old enough yet. I wish I were. I'd be so out of here."

"Things are complicated. But you'll be old enough to do what you want soon."

"I want adventure and romance. And chocolate." She popped another chocolate square into her mouth and offered one to him.

"What kind of adventures?" He opened his mouth to accept the chocolate.

Ava looked into his eyes beneath dark eyebrows. His hair poked out from under his baseball cap. She'd be sad to see him leave the inn, but she had to stick to her plan. Only her plan would bring her freedom and power, so nobody could ever tell her what to do again. She wanted luxury and extravagance and all the finer things in life. She was tired of being poor and being at someone else's beck and call. If the crazy plan she and Agnes had concocted fell through, then she would find another way. She had to.

"Adventure?" she repeated. "I want to have all kinds of adventures. I hate waiting for my life to begin."

"I'm sticking to my island idea," he told her. "I want to live in a small community of friends. We'd build some little cottages on my island and have fruit trees and a vegetable garden and live a simple life. I'd lie in my bed at night and look up at the stars."

"That sounds nice," she said.

What would it be like to lie beside him and look up at the stars in the night sky, listening to the waves?

"I want to have bonfires on the beach at night with my friends, laughing and telling stories," he continued. "And it'd be great to find the perfect partner to do that with."

Ava felt a little twinge. The chocolate was gone. She stood up. He stood up.

"Do you have to go?" he asked with disappointment. "I enjoy talking with you."

"I enjoy talking with you," she admitted.

Ava started toward the door, and Kent took her arm and pulled her to him. Before she knew what was happening, he had kissed her.

"Chocolate kiss," he whispered.

Then he kissed her again, and she felt the room spin and her knees go weak.

~~~

Ava stood outside the gates of the royal gardens, gripping the dogs' leashes. The roses were a vivid rainbow of colors amid the greenery within. She gazed at the castle with longing. She knew she shouldn't let anything distract her from her dreams. Yet she felt irresistibly drawn to Kent.

She touched her lips with her fingertips, remembering his kiss. It sent a shiver of excitement through her. But where would that get her? He had dreams he'd never fulfill and nothing to offer her. He
~~~

was obviously running away from something. Maybe responsibility. Maybe growing up. Maybe trouble.

She spotted Orville perched in a tree right inside the gates. He saw her and whistled a quick message.

"What?" she said out loud. "Are you sure?"

He whistled again and flew off.

Oh, my gosh. She turned and jogged back to the inn, pulling the dogs behind her. She hoped Agnes was in her room. Luckily, Hazel was in the office, and she quickly deposited the dogs and ran up the stairs. She knocked urgently on Agnes's door.

"Agnes," she said into the door. "Let me in. Hurry. This is important."

"Hold your horses," Agnes called out. "I'll be right there."

The door finally opened and Ava fell into the room.

"Geez. What's going on? I was in the restroom." Agnes pushed the door closed.

"You won't believe what Orville just told me," Ava gasped. "I can't believe it. I knew something would ruin our plans."

"Hold on. Calm down and catch your breath. What happened? Just tell me."

Ava stood for a moment, breathing heavily. "Orville told me that the reason they're talking about canceling the ball is because the Prince has been kidnapped."

"No way!" Agnes exclaimed. "How could I not know this? My source isn't very good."

"Obviously, they can't have the ball without the Prince." Ava sat on the unmade bed feeling miserable. "This ruins everything."

"Don't worry, kid. They'll just pay the ransom and be done with it," Agnes assured her. "I just hope they can do it in time for the ball."

"Has this happened before?" Ava asked with surprise.

"These things happen all the time." Agnes waved her hand flippantly. "They just keep it out of the press."

"Can you use your magic to find out where he is?" Ava asked hopefully. "Then we could rescue him, and it would get us in good with his family."

"I'm not telepathic." Agnes frowned. "Ask your friend, Oswald, to fly around and look for anything suspicious."

"Orville," Ava corrected. "Do you think they'll hurt him?"

"Nah. He's too valuable. Unless..."

"Unless what?" Ava asked anxiously.

"Unless they can't pay the ransom. Maybe the royals are short on cash and the kidnappers are asking too much."

"How much is too much?" Ava asked.

"That's the thing. Who knows how much those crazy royals have? Whenever they raise taxes, it's a sure sign they're going broke."

Ava felt a little guilty for feeling attracted to Kent while the Prince was being held prisoner somewhere. Why couldn't anything ever work out? She should probably avoid Kent for a while. But then why couldn't she have a friend? It felt nice to have someone she could talk to besides Agnes. Then again, what good could come of it? She needed to stay focused on what was really important. The Prince.

8 Royal Therapy

"Sometimes people or things get in the way of your dreams. There are always obstacles, and those obstacles test your determination to achieve your dreams," Princess Ava told Jill. "I always knew what I wanted. I felt it was my destiny, and I had to achieve it."

"You mentioned obstacles," Jill said. "What obstacles did you encounter?"

"Well," Princess Ava looked down at her lap. She cleared her throat and looked back up at Jill. "You know about my stepmother. She always thought I was a colossal failure and took every opportunity to tell me so. I had to overcome a lack of confidence from that constant negativity, and then I had to win over my in-laws as well. They wanted the Prince to marry someone from a good family. And... there are always people who try to distract you from your goals." She stared into the distance for a moment. "Let's face it. The odds were against me, but I believe it was meant to be. The Prince and I were meant to be together despite circumstances. We found each other, and I think that destiny always prevails. You just have to believe."

"You were a very determined young woman," Jill commented. "Do you have any advice for young women?"

"I know it's a cliché, but always believe in yourself and follow your heart." Princess Ava placed her hand over her heart.

"Good advice." Jill wrote on her notepad and then looked up. "Let's continue your story. You met the Prince at the ball, and the two of you felt a strong connection, but then you were afraid that his parents would find you unsuitable so you returned home discouraged."

Princess Ava nodded. "The whole evening had

been overwhelming. The ballroom was so beautiful and extravagant, and dancing with the Prince had been a dream come true. I just couldn't process it. I hadn't thought about what to do beyond that point."

"You were so young," Jill stated.

"Yes. I was just seventeen and very naïve. I'd never been out of this town. I'd never had a boyfriend. I felt sad because I was sure that he and his parents would choose one of the other young ladies," she explained.

"So you didn't know he was looking for you," Jill confirmed.

"No, not at first. I felt hopeless and convinced myself that I'd imagined the attraction between us. Why would he choose me out of all the other pretty girls? Even when I heard he was looking for someone he'd met at the ball, I didn't believe it could be me. I couldn't believe I'd be that lucky. I'd had nothing but bad luck my entire life."

"When did you realize he was looking for you, and how did he find you?" Jill asked.

"My father came home from work one day and found me in my room moping. He told me I had to go to City Hall and have my picture taken because the Prince was looking at photos to find some mystery woman he'd met at the ball."

"Did he know you'd gone to the ball?"

"He knew, and maybe he had a feeling that I was the mystery woman. I don't know, but he was very insistent that I go have my picture taken."

"So you had your picture taken," Jill assumed.

"I went down to City Hall, and there was a long line. I felt discouraged and just walked away. I wandered in despair and found myself at the castle gates. I just stood there looking wistfully at my lost dream. I walked around the big wrought-iron fence, staring into the gardens and thinking about my mother. She would've been so proud if I'd lived there in the place we used to enjoy together. I felt so sad and lost. I didn't know what to do. I just sat on a bench outside the gates and cried," she recalled.

"What happened then?" Jill asked, becoming drawn in to the story.

Princess Ava smiled. "He saw me. He was strolling alone through the gardens, wondering if he'd ever see me again, believing that he'd lost me that night. He knew nothing about me. Not even my name. He thought he'd never see me again. He was struggling with his own heartache."

"Go on," Jill encouraged.

"He heard me sobbing and saw me. He didn't realize who I was at first. He was going to send for a guard to see if I was okay, but then he realized I looked familiar. He came closer, trying not to let me see him, but I sensed him and looked up."

"Then what?"

"I stood up, and we just stared at each other. I couldn't believe it. He asked me if I'd gone to the ball. Then he asked how many times we'd danced together. Then he asked my name and told me not to move. He got the guards to open up the gates, and he came out and swept me into his arms. He said he never wanted to let me go." Princess Ava dabbed at her eyes with her handkerchief.

"That's a beautiful story." Jill sighed.

"Sometimes dreams come true."

"So was the glass slipper thing just a myth?" Jill asked.

"People have taken our story and rewritten it and fabricated some things, but I don't mind. The basic story is true. I lived it. I want your readers to know that love and romance are real and that happily ever after is the true ending to this story."

Jill smiled. "Okay. Tell me about courting. How did it work? Did you and the Prince go on dates? How did you get to know each other? There must've been some protocol."

"We went on chaperoned outings. I had dinner here many times. We spent time in the library because we both love to read and spent hours talking about books. We also took a lot of walks around the gardens because we didn't need chaperones when we stayed within the gates. We talked a lot, and the more we talked, the more we knew how perfect it was."

"How did his parents react?"

"They were resistant at first. The Prince was breaking tradition by not marrying another royal, but they came around as they got to know me and realized how happy their son was. Prince Kellan's happiness was the most important thing to them," Princess Ava answered.

Jill glanced up. "Here they come now."

They stood as Queen Aurora and King Kellan slowly approached from the cobblestone garden path. Sarah and Susan trailed behind them.

"How were the roses, Mother?" Princess Ava asked her loudly.

"Lovely. Just lovely, my dear," the Queen responded.

The King and Queen hobbled over and sat beside the Princess.

"That was a long way," the King commented out of breath.

The Queen's head nodded and then snapped up. "Kell? Where's Kell?"

"I'm right here." The King patted her hand.

"No. I mean little Kell." She turned to Princess Ava. "He always hides in the gardens."

"Yes, he likes the gardens," she humored her mother-in-law.

Queen Aurora stared at her. "Are you the nanny?"

Princess Ava sighed and shook her head. "No,

I'm not, but Kell's inside. Would you like to go see him?"

"Don't be ridiculous. It's too cold for a swim," the Queen said.

"No. No. She said do you want to go inside," King Kellan said. "Maybe I'll take a nap."

"Don't take mine," Queen Aurora blurted. "Get your own."

"They can't hear very well," Princess Ava said to Jill.

"Who fell down the well?" Queen Aurora asked, stricken. "Don't just sit there. Call the fire department."

"Where's the fire?" King Kellan looked around.

"There's no fire. Everyone's fine," Princess Ava assured them in a loud voice.

"That sounds nice. I'd like some wine," the Queen said.

"I'll have a brandy," the King piped up.

Jill gathered up her things and put them in her bag. "I should probably go. I've taken up so much of your day, Princess. I appreciate your time. Would it be okay if we continued tomorrow?"

"Of course." Princess Ava smiled graciously.

"I'll come back around the same time, if that works for you, Princess."

"Yes. I'll see you tomorrow, Jill." Princess Ava looked over at Sarah. "Can you show her out, Sarah?"

Sarah jumped up from the bench. "We can go out through the gardens."

"It was very nice to meet you." Jill clumsily curtsied for the King and Queen. They looked at her blankly.

Jill's thoughts were racing as she got into her rental car outside the gates. She was eager to meet the Prince and interview him if he agreed. It would give her a more balanced perspective of past events. Things sounded too perfect. Something told her there was more to the story. Was she being too suspicious? People didn't always have ulterior motives. This might be exactly what it seemed—a simple puff-piece.

She drove to the Quimby Bed & Breakfast in town. She was glad she'd packed an overnight bag, just in case. She'd hoped to get the story in one interview, but now she realized she had to dig deeper.

The B&B was cozy and quaint, just as you'd expect in a small town. She ascended the wide steps and crossed the porch dappled with late afternoon sunlight entering the bright lobby. The wooden floor creaked under her steps as she walked up to the counter. Lacy curtains framed the long windows and wallpaper with tiny flowers adorned the walls. A large portrait of a stern woman with white hair holding two small dogs on her lap hung on the wall.

~~~

Princess Ava was peeved. She hadn't wanted Jill to see her in-laws. It was humiliating and revealed cracks in the façade of her perfect life. They had spoiled the image she was so diligently constructing for Jill. She'd specifically directed the staff to keep her in-laws away from the interview. It was very important to maintain the fantasy. Life wasn't perfect. Love wasn't perfect. But she'd always protected the fairy tale because she believed so deeply in it herself.

She'd completely lost track of time as she'd become engrossed in conveying her version of the story. She glanced at the grandfather clock as she hurried along the hallway. The castle was riddled with grandfather clocks. The Queen loved them, but
~~~

Princess Ava was sick of the incessant ticking and chiming. You'd think with all these clocks, she'd never be late.

She stopped and took a deep breath before she stepped into the room. Prince Kellan was waiting on the flowered loveseat. He was handsome in the way you'd expect him to be. His dark hair had streaks of gray, and he wore his usual ruffled dress shirt and slacks. Dr. Tucker was in his dark wood chair with the matching flowered cushion. He wore his usual navy-blue suit and a blue and gray tie. He had no imagination when it came to fashion.

Princess Ava preferred a female therapist whom she felt would better understand her desire to protect the happily ever after image. But Kellan had insisted on Dr. Tucker, whose family had served the royal family for generations. He believed Dr. Tucker would be more discrete.

"You're late," Prince Kellan accused.

"I lost track of time." She plopped down next to him.

"You're always late," the Prince said impatiently. "How can you be late with all these clocks around here?"

"There are no clocks in the gardens," she said defensively.

"Now, let's not get off on the wrong track today," Dr. Tucker interjected. "We'll pick up where we left off last time and let's work on seeing the other person's point of view."

"You know I'm not happy about the interview," Prince Kellan said to her. She noticed he was leaning away from her on the loveseat. She hated when he pulled away from her.

"I told you; they called me. I didn't call them." Princess Ava looked down at her hands. Her nail polish was such a pretty color.

"And look how you're dressed. Does that woman

know that most of your jewelry is fake?" he asked.

"Kellan," she said patiently. "All I want to do is give people hope for their own happily ever after. You don't understand because you've never lived out in the real world. Life is hard, and I just want people to have hope and believe in their dreams. What's wrong with that?" She looked at Dr. Tucker for support.

Prince Kellan shook his head. "You live in a fantasy world, and you want all of us to enable that fantasy. I'm not going to pretend. We're real people, and we have problems just like everyone else."

"No, we don't." Princess Ava shook her head. "We have a wonderful, perfect life. We *are* living happily ever after."

Prince Kellan sighed heavily.

"How do you feel about what Ava just said?" Dr. Tucker asked.

"I feel frustrated," he admitted. "She wants everything to be perfect, including me, and I can't live up to that."

"What's wrong with wanting romance?" she asked. "Every woman wants romance."

"She reads those stupid romance novels," he said to Dr. Tucker. "No man can compete with those books."

"But you *are* my Prince," Princess Ava protested. "I did marry a prince and I am living in a castle. We are living a fairy tale life."

Prince Kellan groaned.

"Put it into words," Dr. Tucker reminded him.

"She wants me to perpetuate this romantic fantasy she has of what our lives are supposed to be, but she doesn't consider what I want."

"Good," Dr. Tucker said. "Now tell your wife what you want. Remember, we're not mind readers. We have to tell our partners what we want from them."

"I know what you want," Princess Ava said. "You want what every man wants, which is fine, but I..."

"I know." Prince Kellan held up his hand to stop her. "You want me to be romantic. You want candles and music, and you want me to say certain things. It's exhausting. Besides, that's not all I want."

"Go on," Dr. Tucker encouraged.

"I just want to be myself." He looked into Princess Ava's eyes. "I'm not a character in one of your books. I want you to accept me the way I am. I want you to accept reality. I don't want you to obsess about keeping up this perfect image that's false."

"It's not false," she retorted. "Look at me. I'm a beautiful Princess, and you're a handsome Prince. People don't have to know every detail of our lives. It's up to us to set the standard for the perfect romantic fairy tale."

Prince Kellan shook his head. "I can't imagine the story you're spinning for that reporter. Hasn't it occurred to you she's a reporter, and she'll find out the truth?"

"I am telling her the truth," Princess Ava asserted. "Sort of."

~~~

Jill breathed in the morning air. It smelled so fresh amidst the plants. Sarah had brought her straight out to the gardens and had set up a table with various pastries, tea, and coffee. The sun was dissipating the early chill of morning as dew glistened on the surrounding plants. It was quiet except for the chirping of birds.

Movement caught her eye. An iridescent peacock strutted into view and she held her breath. It posed majestically for a moment and then crossed the path and wandered back into the foliage. That's when she noticed another one further away. She rummaged for her camera in her bag, but the peacock was gone by the time she'd turned it on. What a striking picture
~~~

that would've made. She hoped to see them again.

Jill stood when she saw Princess Ava approaching. She waited until she arrived at the benches before she curtsied.

"I saw the peacocks, Princess," she told her with excitement.

"I'm so glad. Aren't they beautiful? And what a lovely morning," Princess Ava said as she settled herself on the bench. She wore a lacy, pale pink gown with a cream shawl around her shoulders. A small tiara sparkled in her hair.

"Yes, and it's so peaceful," Jill answered with envy. "You're fortunate you can enjoy this every day."

"I just love the gardens." Princess Ava looked around. "I hope you had a nice evening in our little town."

"I did. I stayed at the Quimby Bed & Breakfast. It's very quaint and cozy. I guess it's been there a long time. It was very convenient because it was within walking distance of the stores and the library." She reached for a pastry on the tray.

Princess Ava had stiffened a bit. "Good. Glad you liked it."

"I don't want to waste too much more of your time. You've been very generous with me, and I appreciate it," Jill said. She looked down at her notepad. "There are a few more things I'd like to cover, and I was hoping to have time to interview the Prince." She looked up at her.

Princess Ava forced a smile. "I'm sure he'd love to talk with you but, unfortunately, he has obligations today."

Jill nodded. "I'd like to interview the two of you together, if that's possible. I think our readers would love it, and we can get a few photos for the magazine. I guess I could stick around for another day or two if I have to."

"I'll have to check his schedule," Princess Ava

said. She doubted she could convince him. He was so uncooperative. He knew how much this meant to her. Why did he have to be such a jerk sometimes?

"Is something wrong, Princess?" Jill asked at her expression.

"Oh, no. No." Princess Ava laughed lightly. "He's just always busy with so many important projects. I don't know when he'd have the time..."

"What kind of projects?"

Suddenly it occurred to her that this was the answer. She could persuade him it'd be a good way to get the word out about saving the environment and his other futile ideas.

"The Prince has always been interested in the environment and reducing pollution." She attempted to appear sincere. "He collaborates with other countries on solutions for things like overpopulation and poverty. He's concerned about world hunger. We even recycle here in the castle. We have an organic garden and compost our food waste too." She smiled, pleased with her answer.

"That's wonderful," Jill enthused. "I'd like to talk to him about his work. It'd be great for our readers to know about all the good things he does. I know they also wonder what you do with your time. What's a typical day like for you, Princess?"

Uh, oh. She'd sound frivolous if she told Jill that she slept late, read romance novels, watched romantic comedy movies, sorted her jewelry by color, shopped, and avoided her in-laws.

"Well, I'm involved in the Prince's projects, of course. We're both passionate about doing as much as we can." She used her sincere voice again. "I spend time with my in-laws and keep up on the news, so we can be of service wherever we can. I'm also in charge of the staff here. I'm really quite busy."

"I'm glad to hear you and the Prince are concerned with things outside the castle," Jill said.

"It'd be very easy to insulate yourselves from the outside world and the problems of ordinary people."

"That's true, but you must remember that I wasn't born a royal, so I'm not as far removed as some might be."

"That's a valid point." Jill looked down at her notepad. "I think we left off right after you started courting." She looked up. "That's an old-fashioned word, but I assume that would be the case in your situation."

"Absolutely," Princess Ava agreed. "Things had to be done according to tradition, and his parents wanted to take their time getting to know me before they'd approve of the marriage."

"Obviously, that happened. So what was next?"

Princess Ava beamed with satisfaction. This was the part of the story she couldn't wait to tell.

"He proposed right here in the gardens at dusk. We were strolling hand-in-hand, and we came to a cobblestone clearing with a fountain. There are so many lovely fountains here. All these lanterns had been strung around it. It was so pretty. Before I could think about what was happening, he dropped down on one knee. He took out this beautiful ring that had been in his family for generations."

She held out her left hand. The enormous stone was pale pink and was surrounded by smaller multicolored gems. The band was engraved silver.

"Stunning," Jill commented. "What did he say?"

"He said he couldn't imagine life without me and that we belonged together. He'd already spoken with my father. Then he asked me to marry him and slipped the ring onto my finger." Princess Ava dabbed at her eye with her pink handkerchief. "It was the happiest day of my life."

~~~
~~~

"Please, Kell," Princess Ava pleaded, glancing at Dr. Tucker, hoping for his assent. "She really wants to interview you and take our picture. She's coming back tomorrow."

"I told you," Prince Kellan said with irritation. "I'm not interested in promoting your silly, romantic story about our lives. Is this why you wanted an extra session today?"

"Explain your reservations further for your wife," Dr. Tucker coaxed.

Prince Kellan glared at her. "You're feeding people a fantasy. It gives them unrealistic expectations. We're real people with problems, just like everyone else. We're not some magical, perfect couple. Why can't you just tell her the truth and be yourself? Our lives are not so bad. Just be honest with her."

"So what if I'm stretching the truth a little?" she said. "Do you know how many romantic stories have been written based on our lives? Do you really want me to ruin those stories for everyone?"

Prince Kellan shook his head in frustration and turned to Dr. Tucker. "I don't know how to make her understand."

"I understand," Princess Ava said sadly. "You think people shouldn't have dreams."

"That's not what I said at all, and you know it," he objected.

She sighed, and they were both silent for a moment. Why couldn't he just humor her and do this one little thing to make her happy?

"You hear each other, but you're not listening to each other," Dr. Tucker observed. "I'd like you both to try to see the other's perspective. You each have valid points. Can you think of a suitable compromise?"

Just then Princess Ava remembered her idea. Of course! It was the perfect solution that had almost slipped her mind. How could he refuse to do something that would promote his work? She was pleased with herself for coming up with this brilliant resolution to her dilemma.

9 Money Honey

"Let's take a walk," Ava suggested to Kent. "It's stuffy in here, and it's nice and warm outside."

"The chocolate will melt," he said as they sat at the table in his room.

"Come on. You can walk the dogs with me. I have to walk them, anyway," she cajoled. She was tired of being in this darkened room. It felt claustrophobic. "Let's get some fresh air."

"I don't want to go out," he told her. "I'd rather stay here. It feels like our own private world."

"Okay." Her resolve to avoid Kent had dissolved. He was there. What could she do? She felt comfortable with him, and he was easy to talk to. And there was no denying she liked him.

"What's the deal with your parents?" he asked.

Ava never talked to anyone about her parents, but Kent was different. "My father is really nice. I don't know why he's involved with Hazel."

"He could be lonely."

"I guess." Ava shrugged.

"What happened to your mother?"

"She wasn't happy in this little town." It was uncomfortable to talk about. "She fell in love and left my father. They ran off to Brazil. It must've been true love."

"That's why you asked about Brazil."

Ava nodded solemnly.

"Do you ever hear from her?"

She shook her head sadly. "I always hoped she'd send for me, but she probably didn't want my father to be alone. She doesn't know about Hazel. Actually, it was Hazel's husband that she fell in love with."

"Seriously? That's crazy. What a scandal for this town." Kent looked at her with sympathetic eyes. "But that left you in a bad spot, didn't it?"

"My mother doesn't know how bad it is for me.

We were very close, and I'm sure I'll hear from her soon. She's probably waiting for me to be old enough to leave on my own. Then my father can't blame her," she explained.

"You still want to go to Brazil?"

"I bet it's beautiful there," she said.

"I'm sure it is."

"What about your family?"

"My parents are nice people. They just have certain expectations, and I want to be free to live my life the way I want."

"What are you going to do?"

Kent sighed. "That's a good question. I think it's important to live simply and in harmony with nature and for people to get along and respect each other and help those who are less fortunate."

"I don't think you can do all that living on an island," she remarked.

He chuckled. "Yeah. Sometimes it sounds appealing to just run away, doesn't it?"

Ava nodded, thinking about her mother. She got up to throw away the chocolate wrapper, and he got up and stretched.

"These chairs are uncomfortable after a while," he said.

Kent crossed the room and sat on the bed, propping a pillow behind his back. The sound was muted on the TV, and he picked up the remote and flipped channels.

"Hey, this is a good movie. Have you seen it?" He turned the sound up.

Ava crawled onto the bed and sat cross-legged. She wondered how long she could get away with staying in his room. Hazel was probably wondering where she was, but she didn't care. She just wanted to stay right here.

"It's just starting," he said. "I can't remember the name. It's the one where they meet and get separated, and he gets arrested because they mistake him for somebody else. Then she's looking for him, and these bad guys are after her and she doesn't know why."

"Is it a drama?" Ava asked.

"It's kind of mix of adventure, comedy, and romance."

"Romance?" She grabbed a pillow and leaned back against the headboard next to Kent. She hoped he wasn't checking out of the inn soon. It was nice to hang out with someone and have an escape from her dreary life.

~~~

"Where have you been?" Hazel demanded. "I can never find you. What have you been up to?"

"Nothing," Ava answered. "I've just been taking care of the guests. That's all. They always want me to run errands for them."

"Just don't get too chummy with them and let me know where you are." She went back into her office.

Ava had been spending every spare moment in Kent's room. She couldn't help herself. She looked forward to being with him. She could relax and be herself. They ate chocolate and watched movies and had long conversations about their dreams. They laughed and kissed. He made her feel giddy and optimistic and stirred up feelings she hadn't felt before.

The phone jangled at the front desk. She picked it up.

"Can you come up to my room?" Agnes asked. "I need to talk to you."

Ava glanced over her shoulder. "I can't. Hazel's watching me. What's up?"

"You seem to be scarce lately. What's going on?"
~~~

"Nothing," she answered impatiently. "Why does everyone keep asking me that? Do I have account for every minute of my life?"

"All right already," Agnes said. "What shoe size do you wear?"

"Six. Why? Are you making the shoes?"

"No. I was going to ask you to stomp grapes," Agnes said with sarcasm.

"Ha. Ha." Ava rolled her eyes.

"Have you seen your little avian friend, Orwell, lately?" Agnes asked.

"Orville," Ava corrected. "No. I don't have any news. I haven't been outside much. Have you heard anything?"

"No. I hope they don't cancel the ball. I've done so much work on your outfit. I don't want it to be for nothing. Even with magic, it's very time consuming."

Kent came out of his first-floor room wearing his baseball cap and sunglasses. He walked over to the front desk and stood in front of her.

She smiled at him. He smiled back.

"Did you hear me?" Agnes asked on the phone. "I need you to do me a favor."

"I hear you," Ava said distractedly. "What do you want me to do?"

"Promise me you won't forget about me once you make it to the castle," Agnes said. "People are so ungrateful. I just want to be in good graces with the royals again, and you can get me there once you're in."

"Yeah. Yeah. Of course. I've got to go. I have a guest in front of me."

"Okay. Remember, we're in this together. I'll talk to you later..."

Ava hung up the phone. "Do you want to walk the dogs with me? It will give me an excuse to get out of here."

"No." He glanced toward the front door. "I mean,

I don't want to go out today. I have allergies."

"Well, you can't stay cooped up in your room all the time," she pointed out. "You might be allergic to something inside. It'll probably do you some good to get some fresh air."

"I know," he acknowledged. "I didn't mean to stay here so long. I was going to... I should move on soon. I've been trying to figure out what to do, but all I want to do is hang out with you."

"Really?" Ava was happy to hear that.

Kent looked around and leaned closer. "How old are you? I mean, when will you be eighteen?"

Ava looked down at the counter. "A few months." She looked back up at him. "How old are you?"

"Almost twenty." He reached over and took her hand. "I feel so comfortable with you. I can be myself."

"I feel comfortable with you, too," she answered. "I wish you didn't have to leave."

"I know, but I can't hang out here forever." He hesitated. "What if we just took off together? Where would you want to go?"

"Brazil?" That was her first thought.

"That's pretty far," he said. "How much money do you have saved up?"

Ava really wanted to go to Brazil and find her mother. But what if her mother wasn't there anymore? She didn't want to be stuck struggling with some guy. That was exactly what she wanted to avoid. She was trying to get out of a rut and didn't want to fall right back into another one. That wouldn't get her anywhere. The reality was beginning to hit her. He didn't have any money. He didn't have anything. She remembered her mother telling her never to settle. She dropped his hand.

"I have to get back to work," she said abruptly. "I have to go do something for a guest." She came from behind the counter and brushed by him as she headed for the stairs.

"Ava," he called after her. "What's wrong? Let's talk about this later."

She ran up the stairs and knocked on Agnes's door. "It's me," she said.

Agnes opened the door, and Ava stomped in and paced with agitation. How could she have let some guy with nothing distract her like this?

"All right," Agnes said. "You can see them."

She picked up the bejeweled pair of shoes from the dresser. They had low heels and were almost transparent, glittering with blue and silver stones.

"What do you think?"

Ava stopped and studied at them. "They match the dress perfectly."

She began pacing again. She was bursting to confide in somebody.

"That's it?" Agnes complained. "I did all that work and that's all you have to say? Geez."

Ava turned to her. "The shoes are beautiful. I appreciate it, but I… I have something on my mind."

"There's no reason you can't help me get back into the castle when I'm helping you get there in the first place," Agnes reasoned. "I'm not asking too much."

"It's not that." Ava waved her hand at her. "It's a guest."

"People can be rude to the help," Agnes said. "Don't let it get to you."

Ava went to the window and gazed out at the ever-present castle. "I can deal with rude guests. This guest was very nice. And cute."

"Uh, oh. What happened?" Agnes asked with apprehension.

Ava turned to her. "Nothing. We just hung out." She sighed. "But I like him."

"No!" Agnes said sharply. "We have a plan. Don't mess it up with some guy."

"I won't. But..."

"This is not good," Agnes said angrily. "If you mess this up, I swear I'll turn you into... into... a slug."

"You might as well," Ava snapped. "This whole crazy plan will never work, anyway. I don't know why I let myself get caught up in this far-fetched idea. Besides, you can't have a ball without the Prince."

Agnes took some deep breaths. "Okay. Let's calm down. It can still work. They'll find the Prince, eventually. They're keeping it quiet, so that means they must be on top of it. Either that, or he's already back and everything's fine."

Ava looked wistfully at the gown on the stand. "It really is gorgeous, Agnes. Do you really think I'll get a chance to wear it?"

"Of course you will." Agnes sat down on the bed. "Now I promise I won't get mad. Tell me about this guy."

Ava sat in a chair facing her. "I don't know. I just really like him. We've hung out a few times and talked a lot. I feel like I can really talk to him, like he gets me."

"So, what's his story? What's he doing here? Where's he going? What does he do?" Agnes asked. "Is he passing through or hiding out?"

Ava shrugged. "It doesn't matter. He doesn't have much going on. He asked me if I had any money."

Agnes let out a laugh. "What a little scammer, either that or he's just a jerk." Then she saw Ava's face. "Oh, sorry, kid. I'm sure he likes you too, but you can't waste your time on somebody like that. Not when you have a shot at *that.*" She waved her hand at the window framing the castle in the distance.

Ava felt incredibly sad. How could Kent have asked her for money? She wondered if he'd be able to pay his bill. Why did everyone always let her down? She looked at the castle out the window. Then she looked at the beautiful gown on the stand and the sparkling shoes. She sat up a little straighter as her resolve strengthened. She had to stick to the plan. It was the only way to fulfill her lifelong dreams. She had to forget about Kent.

"You're right," she said to Agnes. "Let's do this."

~~~

Ava stared at Kent's door for the next few days as she worked at the front desk. It was all she could do to keep from knocking on his door or calling his room to hear his voice. She missed him. He must've known he'd upset her because his door remained closed, and he didn't call her at the desk. Then she worried that something was wrong. Had he'd actually gone out and not returned? Perhaps he wasn't even in his room all this time.

A box of chocolates was delivered to the front desk. She read the card with hope, but it was for a guest. She could never see another piece of chocolate without thinking of him. She thought about him all day, anyway. She couldn't stop. Finally, she couldn't stand it any longer.

"Walk the dogs," Hazel told her as she handed her the leashes.

"Have you seen that guest?" Ava tried to sound casual. "You know, the guy with the baseball hat that..."

"Why?" Hazel demanded.

"I don't know," Ava stammered. "I haven't seen him lately. I just wondered if he's okay."

"He checked out." Hazel turned to go into her office.

"When?" Ava asked with surprise.

"The day before yesterday," Hazel said over her shoulder.

"Did he pay his bill?" She had to know.
~~~

"Someone came in and paid it for him."

"Who?" she wondered.

"I don't know. A man. Maybe his father. Why?" Hazel eyed her with suspicion.

"I just wondered. He seemed like he didn't have any money."

Ava quickly went outside with the dogs so that Hazel wouldn't see her tears. He hadn't even said goodbye. She felt crushed and suddenly empty. Where had he gone? Had he just gone back home? Maybe he'd gone off somewhere to make his fortune so he could return and sweep her off her feet when she turned eighteen. If only.

She saw her squirrel friend, Essie, perched on a tree branch.

"Where is he?" Ava called up to her.

Essie squeaked a response, raced to the end of the branch, and jumped over to the next tree. The dogs barked. Essie didn't like the dogs and apparently had no information about Kent.

Agnes was leaning over the upstairs banister when she returned. "Come up when you get a chance. I have good news," she said with excitement.

Ava returned Elvis and Priscilla to Hazel's office and trudged up the staircase. She shouldn't have been so hasty in dismissing Kent Clark. She missed hanging out with him. But then, maybe he'd shown his true colors when he'd asked her for money. He was just a big, unrealistic loser who'd do nothing more than stoke her dreams. Why else would he hang out here and never leave his room and then sneak out when she wasn't looking? What a wimpy loser.

Agnes was practically jumping up and down with excitement. She pulled Ava into her room and shut the door.

"It's a go," she said, beaming.

"What?" Ava asked impatiently. She wasn't in the

mood for guessing games.

"Cheer up," Agnes said. "He's back."

Kent? How did Agnes know about this?

"This is great. Now you can wear this amazing gown and matching shoes, and I can't wait to get my hands on your hair," Agnes rambled.

"You mean…?" Ava felt a little confused.

"What's with you today?" Agnes put her hands on her hips. "The Prince was rescued, and the ball is coming up. Get it together, kid. We only have a few weeks to work on this."

"Oh." Ava shook off thoughts of Kent. Her entire future depended on the ball. "Okay. What do we have to do?"

"Good. I'm glad to hear you're finally with me. You've been so distracted lately," Agnes said. "So this is the plan. I'll use a little magic to make him notice you, and then you'll use your charm to snag him."

"That's it," Ava cried. "That's the big plan? Do you know how many pretty girls there are in this town?"

Agnes furrowed her brow. "Okay, so you're short on charm. Remember, his parents will watch from the upper balcony. They like to do that. They'll be looking for someone with poise and manners."

Ava groaned. "Whatever."

"No charm. No manners. You're not giving us much to work with," Agnes complained.

"Well, the most important thing is the Prince. How can I impress him? What's he interested in?"

Agnes sat on the bed, frowning.

"Are you kidding me?" Ava exclaimed. "This is kind of important. I have to know what to pretend to be interested in. Haven't you done any research?"

"Guess we have some kinks in the plan," Agnes admitted. "I'll see what I can get out of my source at the castle."

Ava rolled her eyes. Kent was gone, and all she

had now was this implausible plan concocted by a crazy lady. There was no way this would ever work.

10 Bring Your Own Mask

"Ow!" Ava cried out as Agnes pulled her hair into place. "That's attached to my head."

"I can't believe how much hair you have," Agnes said impatiently. She wouldn't let Ava look at herself in the mirror just yet.

The gown fit like a glove. It felt light, and she could hardly resist swishing the skirt around. The shoes sparkled on her feet. Agnes had put makeup on her face and sprayed her with a vanilla-scented body spray.

"I'm hungry," Ava whined as her stomach growled.

"There will be plenty of food at the ball," Agnes assured her.

Ava tried to stand still and not think about Kent. She spent most of her time trying not to think about him. She went over and over everything that had happened in her mind. Should she have reacted differently when he'd asked her for money? Not at all. Of this, she was certain. Why had he ruined it by asking her? She was better off, anyway. She didn't want to end up stuck with some loser. She had to remember that her destiny was to be in the castle. She'd always known it. She'd always felt it. And she believed it now. So why couldn't she stop thinking about Kent?

"Okay." Agnes stepped back and surveyed her. She had a funny smile on her face. "You look incredible, Ava. You'll be the prettiest girl there. You can look now."

Ava slowly turned to view herself in the full-length oval mirror on the stand. She gasped at her reflection. She looked like a sophisticated woman. The dress accentuated her slim figure, the shoes made her a little taller, and the makeup made her look like a movie star. Her hair was swept up with curls framing her face and a gem studded barrette that held it all together.

"The Prince loves vanilla. The body spray will attract him," Agnes said. "Remember to stand up straight with dignity and confidence. It'll draw him to you, but then you have to do the rest."

Ava nodded numbly.

"Now remember what we talked about. He'll be impressed if you seem compassionate. You have to sound sincere. And remember, he likes to read sci-fi books," Agnes instructed.

"That's a lot to remember," Ava fretted. "I don't know anything about sci-fi."

"You don't have to know anything about it. Just get him to talk," Agnes coached. "He likes sci-fi about utopian societies."

"Huh?"

Agnes shook her head in exasperation. "He's an idealist. He wants to end poverty and all that crap."

"Oh." Ava was admiring her reflection in the mirror. She couldn't believe how good she looked..

"Do you think I could be a model if this doesn't work out?"

"You're not going to be a model. This is going to work."

"But what if..."

"Here." Agnes handed her the midnight blue mask.

"I can't put this on. It'll ruin my makeup," Ava complained.

"He'll still be able to see your eyes," Agnes said. "Only take it off if you can get him alone." She appraised Ava with a discerning eye. "Okay, this is it. I'll help you as much as I can. You only have a few hours to get him to fall in love with you. No pressure."

That's when it hit Ava. This was really happening. Right now. Her entire future depended on this one evening. What if she couldn't get the Prince's attention? What if she was too nervous to speak? She could trip and embarrass herself. Her stomach twisted into knots. What if she threw up all over him? She grabbed her stomach.

"What's wrong?" Agnes demanded. "Nerves?" She wavered for a moment. "I'm not supposed to do this... But I think I can remember... I guess I could try."

"Try what?" Ava asked with a grimace.

"Stand up straight and close your eyes," Agnes directed. "I'm going to remove some of your nervousness and give you a dose of confidence. It should last for a couple of hours."

Ava watched Agnes rub her hands together before she closed her eyes. She could hear Agnes murmuring something. She waited.

"There. Open your eyes. How do you feel?"

Ava opened her eyes. She felt a sense of calm settling about her. She straightened and looked in the mirror as she put on her mask.

"I'm ready," she said decisively.

Hazel looked up from the front desk as Ava descended the stairs. Her mouth fell open, and she quickly closed it. Surprisingly, she'd agreed to let Ava attend the ball and then had laughed in her face.

"Where did you get that dress?" she asked. "And the shoes?"

"Agnes is a seamstress, and she has connections," Ava lied.

"Well, it's too bad all that work will go to waste," Hazel said. "They expect pretty girls from all over Wellstonia to be there. The Prince won't even see you in the crowd."

"I'm not worried," Ava responded as she swept across the small lobby.

Agnes suppressed a smile and rushed ahead to open the front door for her.

Ava gasped when she saw what awaited her outside. There was a small, white and gold coach to which two white horses were tethered parked at the curb.

"I thought you'd like it," Agnes said happily. "I'll be your driver, and I'll be waiting for you when you're ready to leave. Don't forget, the magic wears off after a few hours, so you have to work fast."

Ava nodded. She felt perfectly calm.

There was a long line of coaches and carriages waiting to pull up to the entrance to the castle. Ava looked out the window at all the beautiful, young women ascending the wide steps and disappearing into the soft glow of the castle. There was a lot of competition.

Ava followed the throngs into the castle as their voices and footsteps echoed in the cavernous interior. Tables laden with food and drink lined the ballroom with attendants at the ready. Music played in the background, and the lighting was soft. She gazed upward at a balcony hidden by heavy draperies encircling the room. There was an enormous staircase curving down one side. She found a nook of space by it and observed the sea of color and high-pitched voices.

Ava wasn't sure what she had imagined, but this certainly wasn't it. She yawned. An attendant balancing a tray of champagne flutes was weaving his way through the guests. She quickly snatched one and backed into her nook again. She felt better slowly sipping and assessing her competition.

After a while, her growling stomach compelled her to venture over to the food tables. She didn't want to balance a plate, so she chose whatever finger foods she could find that she could quickly pop into her mouth. That satisfied her hunger pangs. She felt warm and more relaxed as she set her empty glass on a table. The music was soothing, and she swayed slightly to it. She wished she could dance. This was a party, and she wanted to dance. She hadn't attended many parties, but she felt she belonged at this one. She felt it in her bones. Destiny was rushing to meet her at this moment. Right here. Right now.

Then the music halted. The din of many voices was jarring and annoying. An attendant appeared beside her, offering a drink. She smiled and shook her head. He looked familiar.

"What's your name?" She leaned toward him to hear his answer.

"Darby," he said in her ear.

Ava looked at him with surprise. "You're on the football team at the high school."

He was one of the popular boys. He'd never even looked her way.

"You look familiar." He frowned at her. "Do you go to the high school?"

"Not anymore," she answered casually. "I just thought I'd come check this out." She didn't know why she felt the need to justify it to him.

"Yeah. I'm just working here tonight," he said.

She suddenly realized the room had gone quiet.

"Welcome, ladies," a voice boomed. "The King and Queen are happy you could join us this evening and thank you for coming. Prince Kellan looks forward to meeting you and hopes to dance with each of you."

Ava looked around at all the eager young women. It would be impossible for him to dance with each of them. There was surely a lot of pressure on him to be cordial and sociable. She wondered if his parents had pushed him into this. Maybe he was off sulking somewhere. Or maybe he was peering out from behind the draperies lining the balcony. She looked up and turned around until her eyes fell on the top of the staircase, and she saw him peeking out. Then she watched him step out from behind the drapes as he was announced.

"Ladies, Prince Kellan welcomes you." There were gasps and the hum of voices, and then all fell silent. You could hear a pin drop.

Ava couldn't take her eyes off him. He was a regal sight with his black mask and small sparkling crown atop his dark hair. His attire was dark blue and black. He stood straight, and his demeanor radiated poise and self-assurance. He had been announced many times before.

He cleared his throat. "Thank you so much for coming," he said in a deep, full voice. "Help yourselves to the food and drinks. I hope you all enjoy yourselves, and I look forward to dancing with you. Let the music begin again."

He started down the staircase, and the crowd surged toward him. Pausing for a moment, his eyes swept over them. Then his eyes met Ava's. They stood motionless, staring at each other. His eyes were solemn as she braced herself for the crushing wave of young women. He smiled at her, and she smiled back. She stepped up onto the bottom steps and held out her hand. And he brushed right by her as she got pushed aside by the crushing sea of bodies and slammed into the banister.

For hours, she watched him dance with many partners. Her side ached from the banister. She ate and drank and prowled the perimeter of the room, searching for a way to get close to him again. But there were none. Had she blown her only chance?

Ava stood in the long line for the restroom listening to the excited chatter around her. She felt defeated and wondered if she should give up and go home. She didn't know what she could do to get his attention again.

She returned to the long buffet tables and picked through what was left. She saw Darby clearing away some empty platters.

"Hey," he said when he saw her.

"Hey," she answered.

"Did you get your turn?" he asked.

Ava shook her head. She looked around for the Prince. She finally saw him standing over by the banister that had injured her, talking to a group of young women. She made her way over and walked around the tight group, trying to find a way in. It seemed impossible, so she edged her way up a few steps to see better.

That was when he looked over, and their eyes met again. He smiled warmly. She became aware of the music as he reached out a hand to her. She remembered Agnes had promised he'd notice her. The crowd made space for them, but she was oblivious to anything but him.

She took his warm hand, and he led her down the stairs and then pulled her tightly to him. He felt achingly familiar. Was it destiny or Agnes's magic?

"You smell good," he said in her ear.

"Thank you, Your Highness," she said in his ear. "I know you don't want to be here."

"Is it that obvious?" he asked.

Ava pulled back to look at him. She smiled and shook her head. "Not at all. I can just sense it."

"I noticed you," he admitted. "I've been watching you."

"Liar," she said with a satisfied smile.

"I saw you talking to that boy with the tray," he said. "You're the only one who was nice enough to speak to the servers. Everyone else has been ignoring them. You standing off by yourself just watching everyone."

"I was bored," she said.

The Prince laughed and then pulled her in tighter. She was glad when the song ended because she had felt dizzy from all the whirling around. But she was sad when he let her go.

"What's your name?" he asked as he looked deeply into her eyes.

She wasn't sure why she hesitated to answer him. She wished they could take off their masks so she could see his handsome face. Turning away, she surrendered him to the crowd that waited, but he pulled her back. He brought her hand to his lips and gently kissed it. It was like slow motion as her hand fell back to her side, and he disappeared into the throng again.

Ava berated herself. She hadn't even brought up his sci-fi books. Or helping the poor. But they'd had a moment. Undeniably. Unless he was having moments with every one of his partners. Was he just being charming?

She found herself back in the nook by the staircase. She looked up the wide staircase, remembering the moment he'd walked down. It already seemed so long ago. She yawned again and scanned the vast room for him, but couldn't spot him anywhere. The crowd was too thick. She should probably mingle, but she had no interest in talking to anyone who might snub her like the girls in high school. She wished Agnes were there. She wondered what time it was and what would happen when the magic wore off.

Something hard and wet hit her neck. "Ow," she said with irritation. There was a small ice cube by her feet. Where had that come from? Another one flew past her face from behind. She turned. Someone was beckoning to her from under the staircase. Was it Darby? Perhaps it was Agnes.

Ava glanced around before hurrying toward this person in the small, hidden alcove under the staircase. Her eyes slowly adjusted to the dark, and she grasped it was the Prince who stood hidden with her.

"They're going to wonder where you are," she

warned. She didn't know what else to say.

"I need a break. I'm sick of dancing." He sounded tired.

She was frozen with nervousness and anticipation and confusion. Thoughts raced away and collided with conflicting emotions.

"What's your name?" He stepped closer.

She turned away. "You looked like you were having a good time."

She felt annoyed with him for all that female attention. How dare he enjoy himself with other women. She shook her head at herself. She had no right to feel possessive. Besides, he probably wasn't enjoying himself as much as he appeared. He had been forced into this by his parents, most likely.

"I feel like some kind of prize," he confessed. "You're the only one who really looked at me. I feel like I know you. There's something between us."

Ava turned and looked at his silhouette and the brightness of his eyes behind his mask in the shadows. Was it simply magic that was affecting him? She felt drawn to him too. He felt familiar in a way. Perhaps true love felt this way. Had she felt it with Kent? She had very little to compare it to. Or was it a temporary spell courtesy of Agnes?

She took a step toward him as she felt the butterflies awaken in her stomach, but a sudden heaviness made her hesitate. Was the magic wearing off?

Ava reached up and put her hand on his face below his mask. She couldn't help herself. He placed his hand on the back of her neck as he pulled her to him and gently kissed her. She hoped he didn't mess up her hair. It could all tumble down if the barrette opened.

"I knew it was you," the Prince whispered in the dark.

What did he mean by that? Who did he think she

was behind her mask? Or did he also sense they belonged together?

Again, she became aware of a heaviness dragging at her. A bit of panic pitched in her stomach with the butterflies. Agnes had warned her not to stay too long. But things were just getting good. How could she leave?

She pulled away. “I have to go,” she said breathlessly.

“No, you don’t. It’s okay,” he answered. “I know it’s you.”

“I think you think I’m someone else,” she said with sadness. It was disconcerting. “I have to go.”

Ava turned, and the Prince grabbed her arm, but she freed herself and hurried toward the exit. What would happen when the magic dissipated? Would her gown melt away and her shoes turn to dust? How humiliating that could be.

Agnes was sitting atop the coach with reins in hand, waiting for her in the night.

“You’re cutting it close,” she called down.

A valet opened the door to the coach, and she hastily slid in. She grabbed the door handle to steady herself while the coach careened towards the open gates. Her heart pounded, and she tried to catch her breath as the Prince’s kiss lingered on her lips. But he had thought she was someone else. How disappointing. She cried at this realization.

“That good, huh?” Hazel sneered from behind the front desk as Ava burst in.

She snorted a satisfied laugh as she locked the door to the office and pulled the dogs on their leashes to the front door. Ava could hear her chortling down the walkway.

Ava lifted the front of her gown and ran up the stairs to Agnes’s room. It was unlocked, and she plopped forlornly onto the bed to wait for Agnes. She couldn’t make sense of what had happened.

"I parked the coach out back." Agnes closed the door behind her. "It'll be gone by morning."

She unfastened the barrette, and Ava's hair cascaded down around her face. Her scalp hurt from having her hair up for so long.

"Let's get the dress off and then you can tell me everything."

Ava kicked off the shoes and stood up. Agnes unzipped the back, and Ava let it slide off her shoulders into a puddle around her feet. She put her jeans and T-shirt back on.

"It can't be that bad," Agnes said. "Tell me everything."

Ava unenthusiastically related the events of the evening to Agnes, who grinned with delight when she told her about the encounter under the grand staircase.

"He likes you," Agnes exclaimed. "This is great."

"He thought I was someone else," Ava said with dejectedly. "I had my mask on, and he thought I was someone else. Don't you get it?"

"I don't know." Agnes shook her head. "Good move, not telling him your name. Now you're some mysterious stranger who left him wanting more. That was brilliant."

"But..."

"He'll be searching for you," Agnes went on. "It's a smart strategy making him work for you. I don't know why I didn't think of it myself."

"But he'll be looking for someone else," Ava said emphatically. "He thinks I'm someone else!"

"I'll see if I can get information from my source," Agnes continued. "Although he never seems to come through. Ask your little avian friend, Orkel. He'll be inconspicuous."

"Orville," Ava corrected. "Aren't you listening to me?"

"Yeah. Yeah. You think there's some other

woman he's looking for." Agnes furrowed her brow. "Do you think he got you mixed up with someone else?"

Ava stood and stamped her foot for emphasis. "That's what I've been trying to tell you!"

11 Prince Charming

Jill was perturbed. She couldn't quite figure out how to write the story. It was superficial and lacked substance. What was the angle? She had to dig deeper, and it was essential to interview the Prince. She'd been able to interview some residents of Quimby, but they hadn't given her anything. She'd also spent a fair bit of time at the library digging up whatever information she could. She'd convinced her editor to let her extend her stay and continue working on the story, so she'd better come up with something. More than anything, she wanted to humanize the Prince and Princess. She was glad she'd gotten to meet the King and Queen. Their memory problems would be an intriguing part of the story, despite the resistance of the Princess.

Jill breathed in the subtle floral scent of the gardens. These early spring days were warm and sunny. How nice and relaxing it was to sit outside here every day. It felt like a different world, far removed from the reality of all the problems on the outside.

She helped herself to one of the delectable pastries on the little silver cart that had been rolled outside. She could've sworn there'd been more cookies on the tray a few minutes ago. She looked around but saw nothing astray.

Princess Ava approached wearing a long dress with a delicate pastel floral pattern. She wore her usual tiara and rings and smiled as Jill stood and curtsied.

"What a beautiful day," Princess Ava observed. "I'm glad you helped yourself." She settled herself on a cushioned bench and reached for a pastry.

"I don't know how you can eat these every day," Jill commented. "I'd probably weigh 500 pounds."

Princess Ava laughed. "Indeed. We eat very well,

but we make sure it's healthy. Even these pastries are made with organic flour and a natural sweetener. The Prince is very particular about his diet."

"Will the Prince be joining us today?" Jill asked hopefully.

"Unfortunately, he has obligations again today. I think he may have some time tomorrow," she answered. "I'm sorry for keeping you in our little town this long. I hope you're enjoying your stay."

"This is a great town. It's so picturesque, almost like a painting."

Jill scanned the pale blue sky dotted with fluffy clouds, the lush foliage and vibrant color of the gardens, the distant verdant hills, and the quaint little town beyond the gates.

"Thank you," Princess Ava said. "I always thought I'd move away when I grew up, but now I can't imagine ever leaving."

"Yes. Well, let's get started."

Jill set up the recorder and took her notepad and pen from her bag. She paged through her notes to find where they'd left off.

"You described the proposal for me," Jill reminded her. "It sounded very romantic."

"It was," Princess Ava acknowledged. "Prince Kellan is very romantic."

"Is he?" Jill looked up at her. "Tell me more about what the Prince is like."

"Oh." Princess Ava thought for a moment. She certainly couldn't tell Jill that they rarely spent time together and that he was always in his office. She also couldn't tell her they hardly ever had a conversation that didn't end in an argument.

"Let me think. He has so many wonderful qualities. As I mentioned before, he has many charitable projects that he's involved with and works on every day. He's very compassionate about those less fortunate, and he always has time for his family.

He loves kids and animals."

"Uh, huh." Jill was writing. "What else?"

"He's well read and keeps up with the news. He has a wonderful sense of humor. And I don't need to tell you he's very handsome." Princess Ava smiled. All these things were absolutely true.

"He sounds just about perfect," Jill said. "He must have some flaws."

Princess Ava frowned. "Well, now and then he snores."

They both laughed. Or at least she assumed he still snored. They hadn't shared a bedroom since she'd redecorated it in pink lace.

"How about the wedding?" Jill asked. "It must've been quite an event for this little town."

"Yes. We opened it to the entire town. We held it in the main ballroom in the castle. It was the only place big enough," she explained. "We wanted to share our happiness with everyone."

"I saw some pictures in the archives at the library," Jill said. "Your dress was beautiful."

"Thank you. I described what I wanted to the designer. I love lace, and I wanted the gown to be a soft cream color. There were tiny pink flowers embroidered on the veil and the lace sleeves of the dress. I had a bouquet made up of flowers from the gardens. The Prince wore a ceremonial tux that was royal blue."

"You were certainly an attractive couple," Jill said.

"The designer did a wonderful job," Princess Ava enthused.

"Tell me about the reception."

"Yes. We had an orchestra for the early part of the evening with ballroom dancing, which was more formal, then we had a band for the younger people later on," Princess Ava said.

"What about the food and the cake?"

"We had a huge buffet with every type of food. Prince Kellan wanted all the food to be of the highest quality, of course. There were ten cakes. All different kinds. It was all so good, but I spent most of my time talking with guests," Princess Ava said. "I hardly had time to eat."

"I can imagine how delicious everything was," Jill reached for another pastry. "Go on."

"The gardens were beautiful. We had lanterns strung throughout the pathways that illuminated the flowers. It was just breathtaking," she remembered. "Then we ended the evening with fireworks at midnight. It was the most magical day."

"It sounds perfect," Jill said.

"It was the perfect beginning to our perfect life together," Princess Ava sighed. If only it were so.

"Your Highness!" Jill jumped up from the bench. Her notepad flipped onto the ground, and her pen rolled away. She hastily curtsied.

Princess Ava turned her head and was astonished to see Prince Kellan approaching, smiling warmly. He wore a light lavender shirt under his royal blue vest. He had turned on the charm, and she was surprised and grateful that he was coming through for her.

"Please be seated," he said to Jill as he sat beside Princess Ava. "I've been looking forward to our interview, Jill."

She picked up her notepad and fetched her pen from the bushes beside the bench. She was flustered. The Prince was gorgeous. She actually felt her heartbeat quickening. It had suddenly gotten so warm out, and her mind had just gone blank.

Princess Ava noticed the effect he had on Jill. She was so used to him scowling at her, she'd forgotten how handsome and charismatic he was.

Jill cast her eyes down at her notepad and turned it right side up. She cleared her throat and coughed. Then she turned red with embarrassment as she looked up at them.

"I'm not really prepared. I mean, I didn't expect you today. Let me find my notes. It will just take me a moment."

"My wife told me you were interested in hearing about my charitable work," he prompted. "This is a perk of being in my position. I have the opportunity to partner with world leaders in a nonpolitical way to achieve some positive changes."

Jill nodded enthusiastically. "Can you be more specific, Your Highness?"

"I'd love to," he answered as if she were asking him to dance. "I think it's important to point a spotlight on the poverty and injustices that cripple humankind and the planet on which we depend for our very survival. And I feel a responsibility because of the luck of my birth to do what I can to improve the world in any way I'm able."

"That's very admirable. Please go on," Jill encouraged.

He leaned forward and looked her in the eyes as he spoke. "I think we can be much more efficient with the earth's resources using newer and cleaner technologies that use more natural sources of energy such as solar and wind power. We must minimize pollution and heal the environment. It's a wonderful privilege to partner with other countries on these crucial issues."

Prince Kellan leaned back and took Princess Ava's hand. She was moved by this gesture. It had been so long since they'd had any type of physical contact. She tried to maintain a steady, supportive smile on her face.

"I believe in living by my conscience," the Prince continued. "It's unacceptable that there's so much suffering in the world. We simply can't allow it as a society. Greed should not be the driving force of the powerful. Everyone benefits when we can all live in peace and harmony with each other and the planet we share."

Jill nodded fervently. Prince Kellan seemed so sincere. It was puzzling because the Princess had struck her as being oblivious and superficial. Had she misjudged her?

She turned to Princess Ava. "What are your thoughts, Princess, and are you involved in these projects as well?"

Princess Ava peeked uncomfortably at Prince Kellan, who had an expression of amused interest.

"My husband is obviously very ambitious. Of course, I agree with him that all these things are extremely important, and my role has been to support him and keep things running smoothly in the castle. Either it's the children or my in-laws who demand so much of my attention." She gave a little laugh and hoped that her answer was sufficient.

"That's very true," Prince Kellan agreed. "The Princess is wonderful at managing the staff and keeping things under control here." He smiled tenderly at her, and she somehow felt she didn't deserve it.

Jill wondered if she was picking up some tension between them or imagining it. She was hoping to get his side of the story and see if it confirmed Princess Ava's version.

"Prince Kellan," she began thoughtfully. "Princess Ava told me how you met at the ball. I'd like to hear your memory of it."

"What can I say?" he said. "We had an instant attraction and connection. We just knew we belonged together. I was very lucky to have found her."

He stood and bowed slightly toward Jill. "I apologize I don't have more time today. I have a teleconference with the Danish Ambassador in a few minutes."

"Oh." Jill jumped up. "But I have so many more questions for you, Prince Kellan. I'd love to talk again."

"I'm sure Princess Ava can answer them. It was wonderful to meet you, Jill."

He leaned down and brushed his lips on Princess Ava's cheek. It made her realize how much she missed him. She longed to be close once again.

Jill fanned herself as she watched the Prince stroll back towards the castle. She'd met many important people, but no one had ever affected her this way. She tried to regain her composure.

Princess Ava breathed a sigh of relief and was glad Jill hadn't had the chance to question him further or hear his conflicting version of events. That would not have gone well.

"It's gotten warm out here, hasn't it?" Jill settled back down on the bench, still fanning herself. "Your husband is quite gracious and wonderful and seems just about perfect. You really did marry your Prince Charming."

"Yes, I did," Princess Ava answered wistfully.

How had their storybook romance turned so rancid? How had he come to resent her so? And how was she going to spin the story of their children?

~~~

"Kellan?" Princess Ava poked her head into his office.

"What?" he said with irritation at being interrupted.

He had taken off his vest but was still wearing his lavender shirt as he squinted at the computer on his massive desk.

She entered the room and stood until he looked up. "I just... I just wanted to thank you for speaking with Jill today. I really appreciate it. I didn't think
~~~

you were... I didn't expect it."

"It gave me the opportunity to bring up the things that are important to me, even though that's not what she wants to write about," he said. "At least it will get some mention, I hope."

"She just wants to write our story," Princess Ava said. "It's romantic."

"Don't fool yourself. She's a journalist. She's looking for an angle."

"What do you mean?"

"Do you really think she came all this way to hear some perfect, little happily ever after fairy tale? She's looking for dirt. That's all people want to read. It makes them feel better about their own lives when they see we're not any happier." He shook his head and turned back at his computer.

"Is that why you took my hand and kissed my cheek? To throw her off?" she wondered.

"Nobody needs to know about our problems."

"I just want people to believe in happiness and love and romance. I want them to have hope," Princess Ava said out loud, not expecting him to hear her.

"Why give people false expectations?" he asked.

"But look at us. We *are* perfect. We're healthy. We're still young."

"We're middle-aged," he corrected.

"We're wealthy..."

"Not so much anymore, but I've been investing what's left so I think we'll be okay," he said.

She faltered. "What?"

"That's why I replaced most of your jewelry with copies. I sold the real ones," he said.

"But you told me you were keeping them locked up for safekeeping," she reminded him.

"I didn't want you to panic. You freak out about money."

"How is this possible?" she cried. "We're

supposed to be rich."

"This is exactly why I didn't tell you," he said. "Haven't you noticed that half the staff is gone?"

"Yes, but I thought... I don't know what I thought. I just thought there was a reason and didn't really think about it," she admitted. "I guess I figured we didn't need them because the kids are away now."

"Well, when the kids come back, they're going to have to learn to do chores. I think it'll be good for them. They've gotten too spoiled," he told her. "The least they can do is pick up after themselves and clean their own rooms and bathrooms."

Princess Ava studied Prince Kellan's strong jawline and dark eyebrows as he stared at the computer. Even in this mood, he was incredibly handsome. But when had he become so angry at her?

12 Photo Finish

Ava went back to her life, but she felt more despondent than ever. She cleaned. She fetched things for guests. She let Hazel's remarks roll off her. She waited for news from the castle. Surely, there would be an announcement any day of the Prince's engagement. Then she'd know for sure that her dream had died. Truth was preferable to the torment of unrelenting hope. Hope had flitted off to curse someone else now.

"Cheer up," Agnes told her. "These things take time."

Indeed. An announcement came from the castle, but not what anyone had expected. The Prince had met someone who had sparked his interest, but he knew not who she was or her whereabouts.

Ava felt the flutter of hope, but she couldn't let herself get sucked in again. He'd mistaken her for someone else. That she knew for sure. She could continue the charade, but she couldn't pull it off forever. She wished she knew who this mystery woman was. It was hard to impersonate someone you knew nothing about, even though she'd unwittingly managed this feat before. She wracked her brain, trying to figure out how to turn this opportunity her way. It was exhausting.

"Maybe it's you," Agnes said. "Why not? You said he kissed you. That must've been some kiss."

"He thought I was someone else," Ava said forlornly.

"Maybe not. He might've known it was you," she reasoned.

"But he doesn't know me. How could he know it was me if he doesn't even know me?" She looked out the window of Agnes's room at the castle. "Do you have any idea who it could be? Does he have some secret crush on his tutor or something?"

"This whole thing doesn't make any sense," Agnes said from behind her. "Why would they have the ball if he were already interested in someone?"

"Maybe his parents don't like her. He could've agreed to the ball to prove that there was no one else he'd like." Ava faced Agnes.

Agnes suddenly let out a guffaw. "Of course! It's a P.R. stunt. Just like the kidnapping. Those royals know how to generate publicity."

"You think the kidnapping wasn't real?" Ava asked. "But why would they do that?"

"Oh, so people will forget how bad their lives are and cooperate with the royal family and pay their taxes like good little citizens. Politicians create stories all the time to distract people from their miserable little lives. Why didn't I think of this before?" She shook her head. "I bet there's no mystery woman. Pretty soon they'll announce that they found her, and they're engaged. It's just a stunt."

Ava felt crushed. Once again, hope had slapped her in the face. She moped around the inn. It was absolute torture waiting for an announcement from the castle. Hazel seemed to enjoy her misery, which made it even worse.

This might be the time to think about running away. Now that her dreams had been dashed, she had nothing to lose. She wondered if she had enough money to get to Brazil and find her mother, but whenever she thought about it for long, she became angry at her mother. Why had Ava never heard from her? Had something happened to her, or had she simply turned her back on her former life, including her own daughter? Ava wanted to disappear as well. But where? Where could she start a new life? She wished she knew where Kent had gone. Why did everyone always leave her? It made her so mad.

Elvis and Priscilla were scampering ahead,

pulling her by their leashes. It was a nice day, but Ava's mood was now perpetually dark. They passed The Health Nut, and it made her think of Kent again. She was tempted to go in and buy some organic chocolate. That might lift her mood, but she had the dogs with her so she couldn't go in. Besides, it would remind her of Kent too much, and she was still angry at him. And disappointed and disillusioned. And worst of all, she missed him.

Ava stopped while Elvis lifted his leg on a tree. She heard Essie and tilted her head upward. Essie was motioning at something down the street. Ava noticed a flurry of activity at City Hall. She nodded at Essie and headed in that direction. The castle loomed in the distance against the light blue of the sky with fluffy white clouds dangling perfectly above it. She could see scattered drops of color in the gardens like a painting. It was so tantalizing and elusive, like a fairy tale mirage. She sighed heavily.

Her curiosity propelled her toward City Hall. As she neared, she noticed many young women milling about outside the doors. A line had formed that was at least a block long. There was a sign on a metal stand by the door, and she paused to read it.

All Attendees of the Ball
Are requested
To have their Photograph taken
At City Hall
On May 23
From 1 PM to 3 PM.
Please bring valid ID

Were they still looking for the mystery woman? Maybe it wasn't a publicity stunt. It seemed like they really were looking for someone. The dogs were yapping and nipping at everyone who went by. She didn't have her ID with her, anyway. She just had some tips in her pocket.

Ava rushed back to the inn and put the dogs in the office.

"Watch the front desk," Hazel ordered. "I'm going out."

"But..." She thought quickly. "I have to do an errand for a guest. Right now. It's important."

"What is it?" Hazel stood with her arms crossed.

"I have to get her lunch. She's hypoglycemic. I have to go right away," she blurted.

"She'll have to wait or get her own lunch," Hazel answered, grabbing her purse. "I have a dental appointment. I'll be back in about an hour." She whisked past her and went out the door.

Ava felt panicked. What could she do? Hazel might not get back in time. She picked up the phone at the front desk and called Agnes's room. She tapped her fingers on the wood counter as the phone rang and rang.

She watched anxiously as the minutes ticked by on the clock, the incessant tick tock taunting her. She found her ID in her wallet in the closet and stuck it in her pocket. She drummed her fingernails on the counter. Where could Agnes be? She'd know what to do. Maybe she could stop time or something. Was it even worth all this worry? Could Agnes be right that it was just a P.R. stunt? Why wouldn't the mystery woman have stepped forward by now? Was it possible it was her? It was too much to hope for, but she couldn't help it.

Ava called Agnes's room again. This time she answered.

"Where have you been?" Ava snapped.

"I was taking a nap," Agnes answered.

"Didn't you hear the phone?"

"Yeah. I ignored it because I wanted to sleep. My stomach has been killing me. Those darn bagels. I wish they had gluten-free ones, but they wouldn't taste the same, anyway. It's such a bummer..."

"Agnes," Ava interrupted urgently. "They're looking for her."

"Who's looking for who?" she asked sleepily. "Or is it whom? Whom is looking for whom? That doesn't sound right."

"They're looking for the mystery woman. They're taking pictures of everyone who went to the ball at City Hall today."

"Well, how about that? Did you get your picture taken?"

"I haven't been able to go because I've been stuck here," she whined. "They're only taking pictures until 3:00, and I have to wait until Hazel gets back from the dentist. I don't know what to do."

"Let me think." Agnes yawned loudly. "I'll call them and see how busy they are right now. I can watch the desk, and you can run down there."

"I don't know. Hazel will be furious if she gets back, and I'm not here."

"Who cares? This is more important. Let me call them and see what's going on down there. Talk to you in a minute."

Ava hung up the phone and put her head in her hands. Oh, my gosh! This was so stressful. She was afraid to look at the clock. Could it be possible that she was the one he was looking for? Everything would be ruined if she couldn't get over to City Hall in time.

Ava heard someone come in. The front door closed and footsteps crossed the floor. She sensed someone standing in front of her. She pretended to scrutinize some paperwork on the desk until she could compose herself. Planting a smile on her face, she raised her head.

"Welcome to The Sleep Inn. What can I do..."

Kent stood before her. He wore jeans and a plain green T-shirt, and his usual baseball hat and sunglasses. Butterflies surged in her stomach. Nobody had ever looked so good to her.

"Kent," she whispered.

His head was tilted downward toward the floor. "I kept thinking about what I wanted to say to you," he confessed. "I shouldn't have left like that."

Ava suddenly remembered that she was angry at him. "I can't believe you just took off. You didn't even say goodbye."

Kent looked up at her through his sunglasses. She wished she could see his eyes.

"I had all these things I wanted to say, and now my mind is blank."

"Me, too," she said. "Why did you leave? Where did you go?"

"I went back home," he answered. "It didn't seem like you were really interested in doing the things we talked about, and I didn't want to do them without you."

She leaned toward him. "I *do* want to get out of here," she said. "I've been thinking about taking off, and I'd much rather do it with you." She bit her lip. "It scared me when you asked me about money. I don't want to starve to death or something."

"I'd never let that happen. I promise."

Ava believed him. She so wanted to. The phone rang and startled her. She glared at it but knew she had to answer it.

"The Sleep Inn. Can I help you?"

"It's me," Agnes said. "They can do it if you get over there right away. I'll come right down and watch the desk."

"Uh." Ava looked at Kent, but Agnes had already hung up the phone. "Meet me outside," she told him.

He nodded and went out the door. She heard him go down the creaky wooden steps.

Agnes slowly descended the stairs. "I'm never eating gluten again. If you ever see me with a bagel, slap it out of my hand and jump up and down on it so I can't eat it. Swear to me."

"Yeah. Yeah. I swear," Ava said.

"You'd better run over there. It's almost three. Hurry up and good luck," she said, gripping her stomach.

Ava's mind was racing. Was it worth her time to go to City Hall and get her hopes up? She didn't really believe deep down that she was the mystery woman. How could she be? She'd never met the Prince before the ball. He must have mistaken her for someone else.

And now Kent had shown up again. And he was real, and there was electricity between them that lit up her insides. She hadn't been able to stop thinking about him. Maybe *he* was her destiny, though it bothered her that he had nothing. He didn't even seem concerned about his lack of funds. She didn't want to be stuck with a total slacker. What a terrible dilemma.

Kent was waiting outside under a tree next to the sidewalk. He pulled the brim of his hat lower over his face. She remembered he was sensitive to light. How could he expect to live in a warm sunny climate this way? She headed toward City Hall, and he strode along with her.

"I don't know what to think," Ava said, her mind spinning. "How can I depend on you? How can I believe you?"

"I understand why you feel that way. Just trust the feelings you have for me. I know you feel the same way I do. I can tell."

"What do you want from me?" she asked.

"Ava." He grabbed her arm and turned her to him. "I came back for *you*."

He pulled her to him and kissed her. It was long and passionate and made her feel dizzy. She stared at him in a daze. She was speechless and more confused than ever.

"Let's do it," he said decisively. "Let's take off together. Me and you. Tonight."

"Tonight?" she repeated. "Where?"

"Anywhere you want. Take a chance. Follow your feelings. We can do whatever we want."

She looked down the street toward City Hall. "I just have to... I have one thing to do."

She pulled away from him and ran as fast as she could with her heart pounding.

"Ava," she heard him call after her.

She was so conflicted. It didn't sound like he'd followed her. She hoped he wouldn't disappear again because she really wanted to run away with him. But she was afraid. They hadn't even known each other that long. It was crazy.

Ava was out of breath by the time she reached City Hall and gasped for air. The sign was gone from the sidewalk and no one dawdled. She pulled open the heavy door and entered the air-conditioned building.

"I have to get my picture taken," she told the woman at the information desk.

"It's after three," the woman responded curtly.

"I was working. I got here soon as I could. I ran all the way," Ava said breathlessly.

"I'm sorry. You're late. The photographer packed up."

"We just called," Ava argued.

This couldn't be happening.

"You're late," the woman repeated without sympathy.

"But... I think I'm her. I think I'm the one he's looking for. Isn't there anyone who can take..."

"I'm sorry. The photographer is gone. You'll just have to contact the castle. I don't know what to tell you."

Ava despondently walked outside into the bright

sunlight. She shaded her eyes with her hand and scanned the street, but Kent was nowhere to be seen.

"Did you get there in time?" Agnes asked as she trudged in the front door of the inn. "Never mind. I can see by your face that you didn't."

"The photographer was already gone," she said. "They told me to contact the castle. How do I do that? What if I really am the one he's looking for?"

"See if your bird friend, Orkin, can find out what's going on," Agnes suggested.

"Orville," she corrected automatically.

"Whatever," Agnes said. "I'm going back upstairs. Let me know if you find anything out."

Ava stepped back behind the desk as Agnes slowly ascended the stairs. She was filled with despair. Not only had she missed the deadline to have her photo taken, but Kent had once again vanished. Who knew if either of these opportunities would ever be within reach again? She had to know for sure if she was the mystery woman. An inkling of hope persistently clung to her. If she wasn't, she had to figure out how to escape this stifling town. She couldn't bear to stay here any longer. There was nothing here for her now other than her father, and she hardly ever saw him. He worked all the time and stayed away from the inn. She felt sorry for him, but she had to save herself just as her mother had done.

The phone rang, and she picked it up. It was Agnes. "Hey, I forgot to tell you that someone left you a note. It's on the desk."

Ava looked down to see a folded piece of paper with her name scrawled on it. Was it from Kent?

"Who left it? What did he look like?"

"Some guy left it. How do I know who he was? I didn't even see his face." She hung up.

The message was folded up and taped, and she ripped the paper trying to open it. Her hands were shaking.

"City Hall. Midnight. K."

Ava shoved it into her pocket. What did Kent have in mind? Her stomach once again twisted. It was way too long until midnight. Time was either too short or stretched too long. She'd have to pack some things and sneak out of the house that night. She wasn't ready for this.

She called Information, and they connected her to the castle. Easy as that. Someone answered.

"Uh, I didn't make it on time to have my picture taken at City Hall. I was working, so I was wondering what I can do," she said hesitantly.

The lady on the phone seemed uninterested. "Well, you had two hours to get over there. I don't think they're going to accept any more photos." She paused. "Unless the Prince doesn't find who he's looking for. You can probably just take your own photo and send it over. I don't know if they'll accept it, but that's what I would do."

"Thank you. I'll do that," Ava said gratefully.

She called Agnes's room.

"What?" Agnes answered the phone testily. "I was just falling asleep."

"Sorry. You have to take my picture, so we can send it over to the castle," Ava blurted.

"Geez. Give me a break already."

"Not right now," she assured her. "But I thought we should do my hair the same, so he'll be able to tell it's me."

"We can do it tomorrow. It'll take them weeks to go through all those photos, anyway." Agnes yawned. "There's plenty of time."

"Okay. Feel better." Ava hung up the phone.

She wanted to get her photo to the castle as soon as possible, so she could decide what to do about Kent. She couldn't keep putting him off, or he might leave again. And she didn't want him to know how important this was to her. He'd think she was superficial and frivolous, but being chosen by the Prince was a lifelong dream. Kent was her backup plan. He just wouldn't understand.

13 Seriously Late

Prince Kellan didn't even shoot Princess Ava a look when she rushed into Dr. Tucker's office. She hastily sat next to him on the flowered loveseat.

"Sorry I'm late."

"You're always late," he answered, glaring at her. "It just shows me you're not taking this seriously."

"I am to," she said defiantly.

"Your lateness may indicate your resistance to therapy," Dr. Tucker said. "But let's not focus on that now. I'd like you to arrive on time. Punctuality is important to your husband, and I want you to keep that in mind."

"Fine. Okay. Got it," she responded impatiently.

Dr. Tucker stared blankly at her for a moment, which made her feel uncomfortable. Was her makeup smudged? Was her hair a mess? Was she sweating?

"I'd like you to put into words why you're resistant to therapy."

"I'm not," she answered automatically. "I guess I feel kind of ganged up on. I think a woman would understand me better."

"We're all on the same side here," Dr. Tucker assured her. "We all have the same goal, and we're all here to strengthen your marriage. This isn't about who's right or wrong."

"Except when I'm late," she muttered sarcastically.

Dr. Tucker leaned forward in his chair, and she noticed his pink and burgundy tie. The colors were quite pleasing together. She realized he'd said something, and she'd missed it.

"What?" she said. "Can you repeat that?"

"See how she is?" Prince Kellan said to Dr. Tucker with frustration.

"I noticed his tie. The colors are..."

"What I was saying," Dr. Tucker interrupted, "is

that it's important to listen and hear each other. If you're feeling uncomfortable, then I'd like you to verbalize it. Then we can understand what you're feeling." He leaned back in his chair. "It's important that you feel safe to communicate honestly. There's no judgment here. Just honesty."

Princess Ava shook her head. "Now you're not being honest. The first thing you did was judge me because I was late and make assumptions about it."

"That's a valid point," Dr. Tucker agreed. "Let's continue and move forward."

She felt a bit of satisfaction at his acknowledgment.

"I'd like to thank Kellan again for speaking to Jill, who's been interviewing me. It meant a lot to me," she said generously, wanting to head in a more positive direction.

"Good," Dr. Tucker said with a smile.

"I only did it to bring some substance to the interview," Prince Kellan explained. "I'm apprehensive about how the article will turn out. I don't want us to sound frivolous and removed from reality."

"Why don't you share with us what you and Jill have been talking about," Dr. Tucker suggested to her. "It will ease your husband's fears and help him understand your motivation."

"Well," Princess Ava said. "She keeps asking how we met and about our wedding and my background. She just wants to know our story; that's all. I don't think there's any hidden agenda. People love romantic stories."

"You're so naïve." Prince Kellan shook his head. "I hope you're not making up some big romantic fabrication that she'll see right through, and I hope you're being discreet. Some things are private."

"I know that," she answered. "What I'm telling her is mostly true. I'm not about to tell her we have problems. I don't think we have problems. We don't, really."

Suddenly tears welled up. She wasn't even sure why, but she felt unbearably sad. At one time, all her dreams had come true, and she'd been bursting with joy. She'd married her Prince, and they'd had a dream wedding and been madly in love. And she was trying so hard to hang onto it, but it was slipping away. Where had they gone wrong?

Prince Kellan and Dr. Tucker exchanged puzzled looks.

"Now what's wrong?" her husband asked.

"Why don't you tell us what you're feeling?" Dr. Tucker suggested gently.

"I don't know." She sobbed. "I just don't know how we got to this point." She looked at Kellan through her tears. "We were so happy."

"Go on," Dr. Tucker encouraged.

"I just don't know." She shook her head.

"What don't you know?" Dr. Tucker persisted. He felt they were on the verge of a breakthrough. "Put into words what you're feeling."

"I don't know. I don't know." She took a tissue from the box that Dr. Tucker held out to her and dabbed at her eyes. This was going to ruin her makeup and make her eyes all red and puffy. She hated that they'd made her cry. It made her feel weak and helpless, and now she'd look awful.

"How can I know why she's crying if *she* doesn't even know why she's crying?" Prince Kellan asked impatiently.

"There! That's it!" she cried. "You're always mean to me."

"Am not," he responded.

"Am too!"

"Okay," Dr. Tucker said calmly. "Let's get to the bottom of these feelings."

Princess Ava was glad the focus had shifted from

her lateness to Prince Kellan's anger with her. Dr. Tucker had finally noticed it. Everything wasn't all her fault. She relaxed a little as Dr. Tucker addressed her husband.

"Put into words what you're feeling towards your wife," he directed.

"Nothing," Prince Kellan answered. "Well, I don't mean nothing, obviously."

"Look at her and be honest," Dr. Tucker coaxed.

Her husband shifted toward her. She waited, fretting over what he might say. She didn't know why he was so short with her. It had been this way for a long time between them.

"I guess I do feel pretty frustrated with things," he admitted. "We just seem to have gone in different directions and have different priorities. Maybe we never really knew each other. Maybe we're too different."

Princess Ava didn't know what to say. What was he saying? She looked at Dr. Tucker with dread.

"This is good," Dr. Tucker said. "I hear some genuine honesty. From here we can build a foundation of honesty and acceptance that will strengthen your relationship."

This calmed her rising feeling of doom a little.

"So how do we do this?" Dr. Tucker rhetorically asked. "The first thing you each need to do is decide whether to commit to this process and your relationship. Then you each need to agree to be completely honest with each other. Are you ready to do this?"

They glanced at each other.

It didn't sound fun at all. Princess Ava felt everything was perfectly fine other than her husband's attitude towards her. He just needed to adjust his attitude. She didn't know what she was expected to do. She was the same person she'd always been, so what was the problem?

It may have all started when she'd redecorated their bedroom. He'd complained that it was too feminine and moved into another room. But so what? A lot of couples need their own space. He was the one who'd turned fanatical about all his stupid saving-the-world projects. He was always in his office on his computer, ignoring her. How was that her fault? How could he be angry with her when it was clearly his fault?

He was the one who had insisted on therapy. She could never figure out what it accomplished since all they did was argue in each session. Dr. Tucker merely served as a witness. Now if she didn't agree to take part, she'd be the bad guy. She was really weary of all this introspective bickering. She just wanted to be done with it and back to having a nice husband again.

"I think it's vital for us to find out if we can salvage our relationship," Prince Kellan was saying. "I know it's typical for couples to grow apart, but I think we've gotten to a crisis point. We've just grown too far apart, and I'm not sure that we ever really understood each other in the first place. I don't think we ever had a solid foundation to build a marriage on, but I'm committed to doing whatever it takes."

They turned to Princess Ava. Both their expressions were so solemn that she had to stifle a laugh.

"Yeah. Of course. That's why I'm here in the first place," she said.

"Good. Now we can move forward, and the hard work begins," Dr. Tucker said with enthusiasm.

She thought he seemed just a little too happy at all their misery.

"The first thing we'll talk about is the beginning of your relationship. I want each of you to think about what attracted you to the other person. What was it that drew you and what was it you liked or admired? I'll give you a few minutes to think about this."

Princess Ava noticed the ticking of the wooden clock on the mantle. She saw the sunlight streaming through the windows and longed to be in the gardens. She wondered what her husband would say. Wasn't it always physical attraction that drew you when you were young? Who thought about common goals or interests or beliefs at that age? Things were pretty superficial. They really didn't have to be that complicated, anyway. Did they? Why analyze things to death?

"Okay." Dr. Tucker tapped his fingertips together. "Who would like to start?"

"I remember vividly the first time I saw her," Prince Kellan began. "She was sitting on a bench in the royal gardens with her mother. The sun was shining, and her hair was this golden color in the sunlight, and she just seemed luminous. I was mesmerized. She was the most beautiful thing I'd ever seen, and I vowed to find her." He faced her.

Princess Ava was stunned. "You never told me that," she whispered.

"Go on," Dr. Tucker prompted. "What else?"

Prince Kellan looked at Dr. Tucker and then back at Princess Ava. "There was something so innocent about her when we met. She was in a terrible situation, and I knew she didn't deserve it. I was worried about the expectations of my family, but I thought together we could make the kind of future we wanted." He shook his head. "We used to talk to each other, but I don't feel we can anymore."

"Let's leave out the comments about your current situation," Dr. Tucker suggested. "Ava, what were your first impressions, and what drew you to Kellan?"

She looked into her husband's eyes. Her thoughts raced, clashing past and present feelings.

"He was cute and he was nice to me. He seemed so smart and mature and sincere. I just felt good when I was with him." She shrugged, not knowing what else to say.

"Good," Dr. Tucker said. "What kinds of things did you enjoy doing together in the beginning?"

"I always loved being in the gardens. It was so peaceful," Princess Ava recalled. "Kellan knew the names of all the flowers and plants. I just enjoyed listening to his voice."

"We had books on botany in the royal library," Prince Kellan said. "I spent a lot of time in the library growing up."

"We used to talk about books a lot." She smiled at him. "We both love to read."

"But now all you read are those silly, romance books," he complained. "It's distorted your expectations."

"Let's stick to the past for now," Dr. Tucker reminded him. "I think we did some good work today. I'm going to give you something to think about for our next session. I want each of you to write a list of qualities that represent your idea of the perfect partner and perfect relationship, things such as good communication or whatever is important to you. I don't want you to compare your lists or talk about them with each other until our next session."

Princess Ava felt optimistic about therapy for the first time. She was still savoring Prince Kellan's description of the first time he'd seen her. It was the most romantic thing he'd said to her lately. She'd never known he'd seen her in the gardens with her mother sitting on a bench on a sunny day. His words made her feel warm inside.

14 The Prince or the Pauper

Ava was wide awake and aware of every second as it ticked by on the clock. It was maddening how slowly time moved. The house was quiet. Even the dogs had settled down. She was going to have to climb out the window to avoid waking them. Hopefully, they wouldn't hear her and start barking. The ruckus would rouse her father and Hazel, and she'd be caught.

She wondered what Kent had in mind. Dozens of scenarios played in her head. And she still had the Prince to think about. Agnes had promised to fix her hair and take her picture the next day. What if she really was the one he was looking for? What would happen to her feelings for Kent? She wished she'd never met him. She didn't want him to interfere with her long-term goal of living in the castle. Somehow, some way, someday she'd get there, if not now. It was meant to be. She just knew it, yet she felt drawn to Kent at the same time. No! She mustn't think about him. Oh, she was so confused. She wanted Kent, and she wanted the Prince. She was so torn.

Her stomach churned with anticipation as she slowly opened the window and climbed out. She carefully closed it and breathed a sigh of relief. So far, so good.

The moon was almost full, giving her some light as she hurried along the empty streets. All the houses were dark. She heard a sound and noticed a raccoon ransacking a garbage can. He looked up at her, and she gave him a brief wave. He turned back to his task.

Once she rounded the corner, street lights illuminated the main road. It felt strange to be out so late with no one around. She could see City Hall a few blocks away. The wide front steps were lit, but the double doors hid in darkness. She couldn't see anyone as she approached. Had Kent disappeared on her again? She'd never forgive him if he pulled that again.

But then he stepped out of the shadows wearing his familiar baseball cap.

"I was hoping you'd show up," he said.

Her heart leaped into her throat at the sight of him. She hadn't realized how much she'd longed for him until this very moment. Her will dissolved.

"Kent," she whispered.

"Where's your stuff?" he asked.

He had a backpack slung over one shoulder. He dropped it to the ground on the top step. She walked up the steps to meet him.

"What stuff?"

"Your stuff," he repeated. "We're taking off tonight." He pulled her into an embrace as she reached him. "You feel so good. I missed you."

"I missed you too." She melted into him.

"I guess it doesn't matter," he said in her ear. "We don't need much as long as we have each other."

"I can't leave tonight," she murmured.

"What?" He pulled back from her. "Why not?"

"I... I didn't know that was the plan tonight," she answered.

"What do you mean? We talked about taking off together and doing what we want for once. I thought this was what you wanted. What's stopping you?"

Ava could see the castle over his shoulder. It sparkled in the moonlight. It was mesmerizing, magical. It held her in its thrall. It radiated possibility and tantalized her with fairy tale dreams. Everything seemed possible when she looked at it.

Kent turned to see what she was looking at. His face reflected his disappointment.

"I thought you were different," he said. "You're just like every other girl in this town. You just want to live in that castle and be married to a prince."

"I'm not like the other girls," Ava insisted. "It's not like that. You don't understand." How could she explain it to him?

"It's all superficial. Think about it. Would you rather have love or material things?" he asked her.

"I want it all," she answered defiantly. "Why can't people have it all?"

Some people did, and she wanted to be one of them.

Kent looked at her sadly. "I just want to live simply. Things are meaningless. I want the people in my life to give it substance and meaning, not what I own."

"I've never had anything," she told him sadly. "And I've never been able to count on anybody."

"You can count on me, Ava," he vowed. "We don't need anything. We can be happy together. We just need each other."

Ava wanted so much to believe him, but she couldn't bear the thought of scrounging to survive. Her life had already been so difficult. And the castle glowed enticingly in the distance.

~~~

Ava sat still as Agnes worked on her hair. She thought about her conversation with Kent on the steps of City Hall at midnight. He'd been way understanding. He'd told her he wanted her to be sure and had given her a day to think about it, but her longings continually wavered back and forth.

Kent was sincere, and she absolutely trusted him. He was smart, and he'd figure something out. Adventures awaited. They'd travel and meet different people, and it'd be exciting. Or there would be no money, and they'd end up in some ratty little apartment with nothing, and she'd regret it the rest of her life.
~~~

The Prince was handsome, although she'd only seen half of his face below his mask. She really knew nothing about him. Would they have anything in common? Would he be a self-centered jerk? His shortcomings wouldn't matter if she had everything she'd ever wanted and lived in that beautiful castle and could sit in the gardens anytime she chose. Or would her life be empty, surrounded by beautiful things and bereft of love? Love was important.

How could she make such an important decision when she didn't know what possibilities the future held? The Prince might not even choose her. And then where would she be? Kent could be long gone by then. She couldn't stand the thought of losing him again. How could she bear it? It felt so right when she was with him. It also felt like she belonged in the castle. What to do? She shook her head.

"Sit still," Agnes ordered.

"Agnes, how can you tell when you're in love?"

"Oh, you'll love the Prince. Believe me. What's not to love? He's rich and good-looking. You can't go wrong."

"I know," she said. "But what if I have feelings for someone else? How can I tell..."

Agnes suddenly yanked her hair. "Who? Is it that boy you told me about? Don't let some boy distract you from our plan. I can't believe this."

"Ow." Ava twisted to look at her. "I'm serious, Agnes. I can't help how I feel."

"All right. I can see that." Agnes perched on the bed. "I don't want you to do anything hasty. Let's stick to the plan for now. You can have that boy if things don't work out with the Prince."

"I have to make a decision," Ava asserted. "Or I'll never see him again."

"He's giving you an ultimatum? That's pretty selfish of him. Doesn't he realize the opportunity you have here?"

"Yeah, but he thinks it's shallow. He says love is more important than material things."

"Really?" Agnes raised her eyebrows. "So he says he loves you? Well, if he did, he wouldn't stand in your way."

"I guess he didn't actually say it," Ava realized. "But I'm trying to figure out how I feel."

"What about how I feel?" Agnes demanded. "I've invested a lot of time in this, and now you're ready to throw it all away on some boy who insinuates that he might love you. What about me? We agreed on a plan, and I think you should stick to it."

"You're just using me," Ava accused.

"Get a clue," Agnes answered angrily. "We've been using each other to get what we want. That's the way life is. Get used to it."

"Can't you just be my friend for once?" Ava yelled. "You're supposed to be my fairy godmother. I thought you were on my side."

Agnes sighed heavily. "All right. All right already. Here's my best answer. Why can't you have them both? Have your castle and your boyfriend too. Why not?"

"You mean, marry the Prince and have a secret boyfriend?" Ava shrieked. "He'd never go along with it. Besides, that's not something I want to do. I want true love with the right guy."

"Wouldn't you rather have them both if you could?" Agnes asked. "Think about it. If it were a possibility, it'd solve everything. Together they'd be perfect. You can have the perks and prestige of being in the castle and being a princess, and then you can have your boyfriend to give you romance. Actually, it's brilliant."

"No, it's not. It's messed up. I want to be madly in love and live in a beautiful castle. That's the way things are supposed to be, and that's what I want," Ava said decisively.

"Sorry, kid. That's not reality. Now get over here so I can finish your hair and take your picture. We have to get this done today. I have a good feeling about this. I think you've got a shot at the Prince," Agnes said cheerfully.

~~~

Ava was sitting on the steps of City Hall after midnight. The moon was full this time. She'd always felt a little affected by the full moon. It made her a bit agitated and energetic and unsettled. She was nervous, anyway, because Kent hadn't shown up. Was he just late or had he given up on her?

Were things going wrong? Agnes had some trouble taking her photo because the battery in her camera was dead. Her spare battery didn't work either. Then she'd finally taken it with her cell phone, but she had an old phone and the quality was awful. Ava told her to wait before submitting it to the castle. There was something that was holding her back. Was it Kent? Were her feelings for him screwing everything up?

There was a huge clock on a post outside the doors of City Hall, and she could see that it was almost ten minutes after midnight. A sense of desperation rose within her. She'd finally made up her mind. She couldn't depend on some childhood dream. Her decision had to be rooted in reality. Kent was real and ready to take her away from everything tonight. She didn't want to wait another moment to begin her new life. It was time to change her dreams.

The castle shimmered under the moonlight. What an elusive fantasy. How had she gotten sucked into believing so vehemently that her future was in that distant mirage?

She had the power to take charge and change her future tonight. If Kent showed up. Where was he,
~~~

anyway? Had he stood her up? Had her obsession with the castle driven him away? Again.

Ava glanced over at the castle. It seemed to taunt her. She was glad that Kent had finally opened her eyes. She decided that even if he didn't show up, she wouldn't submit her picture. It was all some silly game. The Prince was toying with them. He was already enamored with some mystery woman, and she would be his choice. He'd never settle for some lowly maid. How could she have been so stupid?

This decision lifted a burden. Now she could focus on her real future and escape this suffocating little town. She wanted to run off with Kent. He was the only one who'd ever really listened to her and cared about her. Together they could have a wonderful life filled with adventure and romance. It was possible they could even make their fortunes. Anything was possible. And if not, at least they'd have each other.

Ava suddenly knew how very important that was to her, but now he seemed to be gone again. How could she find him? She had to find him. She stared at the castle with hate. Had it cost her Kent?

She couldn't bear the thought of going home and crawling back into her little bed alone. She leaned back on her elbows and looked up at the moon hanging low in the sky. Her backpack was on the step next to her. She'd stuffed it with her favorite clothes and all the money she'd saved. It wasn't much, but it was a start. It would get them somewhere.

Ava yawned. A noise startled her. Two cats were running across the street. And then she saw someone walking alone in the darkness. Was it Kent? Of course, it was Kent. Who else would stroll around at this hour?

She watched him walk up to her. He had on a backpack and his baseball hat. The brim of his cap threw a shadow over his face.

"I fell asleep," he said. "I'm really glad you waited."

"I thought you weren't coming," she confessed.

"It looks like you've decided to go with me." He nodded at her backpack and sat down beside her.

"I was so scared that you were gone again," she told him. "But now I'm ready to leave this town."

"What about..." He turned and gestured toward the castle. "I know that's what you really want. I don't want to be your second choice."

"Kent." She liked saying his name. "I just want to be with you. That castle is just a silly fantasy. It helped get me through my darkest days, but I'm ready to leave all that behind."

"But what if the Prince sees your picture and chooses you? You'll miss your chance," he pointed out.

"I didn't send in my picture. I realized I couldn't stand it if you left again. You're the one I want."

"But I can't offer you anything," he reminded her. "We'll have to struggle. I just want you to understand what you're getting yourself into. It won't be easy."

"We'll be together. That's all I want. I've struggled my entire life. I don't know anything else, but at least we can struggle together," she said. "Sure, I'd like to have nice things and an easy life. Who wouldn't? But you're the first person..." She felt tears welling up.

"Oh, Ava." He pulled her into his arms. "I just want you to be sure. I don't want you to regret this."

"I am sure," she said into his shirt.

She felt a flutter of optimism. They were on the cusp of a grand adventure. What would tomorrow and the day after bring? It was exciting and terrifying.

"Ready?" Kent asked her.

She nodded.

They put on their backpacks, and she trailed

after him. They walked a long distance through the cool night air to the outskirts of town. The full moon lit their way, but she couldn't help feeling creeped out by the menacing shadows around them. She followed him with trepidation as he delved into the woods, pointing a flashlight. She was certain she heard the rustling of wild animals lurking around them. They differed from her nice animal friends.

Kent suddenly stopped and kneeled down under a large tree in the shadows. He slipped off his backpack, and she watched as he unfurled a tightly rolled sleeping bag that had been attached to the bottom frame of his backpack. He smoothed it out on the ground.

"We're sleeping here?" she asked with terror.

"I've slept here before," he answered. "This is a good spot. We'll get you a sleeping bag tomorrow. We have to share mine tonight. Luckily, it's pretty warm out."

Ava dropped her small, inexpensive backpack onto the ground. She hadn't been able to fit much in it.

"So, what are we going to do? Are we going to walk every day and camp out every night?"

This didn't seem like a good plan. Camping wasn't her thing. She preferred sleeping in a nice, comfortable bed with no bugs or scary animals around.

"I'm hoping to get a car tomorrow," Kent told her.

He'd unzipped and opened up the sleeping bag. He sat cross-legged on it and patted the spot beside him. She sat down. She wasn't sure what to think. She hadn't really pictured what it'd be like. They had little money, and it wouldn't last long, especially if they bought a car. At least it would get them a good distance away, but where were they heading and then what?

"We might be able to buy a van or something we

can sleep in," Kent said thoughtfully. "Wouldn't it be fun to drive around and see the country and camp out under the stars every night?"

That did sound fun, but what would happen when the weather turned cold?

"Don't worry." He assured her. "It will all work out. We have each other, and that's what counts."

Kent took off his hat and ran his fingers through his curly hair. She'd never seen him without his hat and hadn't realized his hair was so curly. She could hardly see his face in the shadows. An owl hooted, and she scooted next to him.

"Let's get some sleep. We'll make a lot more progress tomorrow."

Kent lay down and pulled Ava down with him. She put her head on his shoulder, and they snuggled together. It felt comforting, but she was wide awake. He kissed the top of her head as she worried about bugs crawling on them. They could be eaten by wild animals or covered by killer ants by morning.

15 Happy High

Princess Ava was still on a happy high after Prince Kellan's words in therapy that morning. He'd described seeing her for the first time with her mother in the gardens. It was so romantic. He was more emotional and sentimental than he seemed. How could she get him to be that way all the time?

"I just love this time of year," she said to Jill. "The flowers are blooming, the days are warm, and the gardens smell so lovely."

"Yes, it is beautiful out here," Jill agreed.

The Princess seemed to glow with happiness today. Jill would certainly glow all the time if she were married to that gorgeous Prince.

"Will your husband be joining us today?" she asked hopefully.

"I don't know," Princess Ava trilled. "Probably not. He's always so busy."

Jill wondered if she'd been wrong. Perhaps Princess Ava's life really was perfect. She was married to a handsome, smart, charming Prince who was also caring and compassionate. She lived in this exquisite castle surrounded by scenic gardens with roaming peacocks in this picturesque little town. How lucky could you get?

"The children," Jill said, looking down at her notepad. "We haven't talked about the children at all. I haven't seen them around."

"The children attend a private school for royal children in Switzerland," Princess Ava informed her. "They're old enough to be away from home. We miss them terribly, but their education is important, and they come home as often as possible."

She didn't want to mention that they spent most of their free time with other young royals in Monaco partying and who knows what else. She'd never been good at controlling them, and it was just as well that they preferred being elsewhere.

"Of course," Jill answered. "I found a picture of them in a magazine from a few years ago. Your son resembles your husband, and the girls look just like you."

"Yes." Princess Ava nodded and fixed a smile on her face.

"Can you tell me a little about each of them?" Jill asked.

"Of course. Our son Prince Kellan Charles is the oldest. We call him K.C. Charles was Queen Aurora's brother's name. K.C. is pretty easy-going and excels at technology. He graduated high school a few years ago and is still trying to figure out what to major in, though he has a good ear for languages. He's our linguist."

"Wonderful. And the girls?"

"Princess Haley Aurora is a few years younger than K.C. She enjoys studying the culinary arts and especially enjoys learning about international cuisines. She also has an ear for languages. She's very creative and quite artistic in many mediums."

"Great. And the youngest?"

"Princess Gwendolyn Agnes is more outgoing and adventurous," Princess Ava said. "She loves the outdoors and enjoys botany like her father. She also loves the ocean and studying marine life."

"It sounds like they each have their own unique areas of interest," Jill noted.

"Yes, they certainly do."

"It must be difficult raising children born into this kind of life. I don't know how you'd keep them from being spoiled and apathetic," Jill commented. "I mean, you were raised in this town, so you can appreciate all you have and how difficult things are for most people. Your children have been sheltered from many of the things that most people deal with."

"Yes, that's true," Princess Ava acknowledged.

"But you can see that my husband isn't apathetic despite being raised here in this castle. He wants the children to see the world as it is with all its problems and use their positions to better it, as he does."

"Good point. Prince Kellan is a wonderful role model for them in that way."

"I'm afraid I'm not as good at educating the children," Princess Ava admitted in a moment of honesty. "I'm better at teaching them manners and etiquette and protocol. These are things we need to know as royals."

"It sounds like you balance each other out as parents," Jill said kindly.

Princess Ava didn't like to think about the children too often. They had gotten a bit out of control ever since they'd been sent off to school. They were probably playing hooky right now. She'd never really wanted to have children, but it had been required that she produce heirs. She'd thought after she'd had a son that that would suffice. However, to her surprise, her husband and in-laws had expected her to have more children. Apparently, Prince Kellan loved kids. So, she'd spent more time than she'd desired being pregnant and supervising nannies.

It hadn't been her ideal vision of life in the castle, but she'd gotten through it and convinced her husband it was best for the children to send them away to private school because they should have the very best education available. It had been her hope that once the children were gone, she and Prince Kellan would have the romantic life she'd anticipated and deserved.

But no! Her husband had moped around missing the children, and her in-laws were constantly underfoot. Then they had declined, and suddenly she was required to spend more time with his parents as he became more immersed in his charitable endeavors. It was the most frustrating thing ever to deal with her in-laws' dementia. And now she had to get her romance fix from her books. Her life was a fairy tale come true, but it wasn't quite what she'd imagined. Who would've thought it would turn out this way? But she was going to make darned sure that everyone believed in her happily ever after. It was the least little crumb of satisfaction she could have.

~~~

Jill had stayed much longer than she'd expected. This little town had grown on her, and she was going to miss sitting in the serene gardens and eating those delectable pastries. She'd also gotten some great photos. Sarah had taken a picture of Jill with the royal couple. She'd positioned herself next to the Prince and was tempted to crop out the Princess.

She wasn't looking forward to getting back to the bustle of her job and busy life. The office was always frenetic with everyone jostling for placement in the magazine. She wasn't sure how this article would turn out, despite being certain she'd gotten all the information she could find in this limited time. Yet she knew there was more to the story. It was obvious the Princess wasn't being entirely truthful, but she needed to get back.

Hopefully, she could piece together a provocative cover story from her research and interviews. Princess Ava and Prince Kellan were obscure royals whose lives had been the basis of a popular fairy tale upon which many young girls based their dreams. Jill had hoped to expose the reality, but it wasn't meant to be this time around. Unless she was missing something.

Still, she questioned how a superficial commoner had snagged the most handsome, charming, humanitarian prince in the world. Had the Fairy
~~~

Godmother bewitched him with a spell? She wished she'd been able to interview the Fairy Godmother, but the Princess had told her she'd retired many years ago and didn't know where she could be found. It was all very mysterious and suspicious, but that could be the cynical journalist in her. Her divorce and lame love life may have skewed her perspective.

Oddly, this fairy tale had inspired her to consider giving internet dating another try. There had to be someone out there who'd appreciate her drive and ambition. Someone who was just as cynical and wounded. Someone who'd appreciate her eccentricities and enjoy opinionated, analytical, passionate discussions late into the night. And share snippets of delusional optimism.

Deep down, Jill wanted to believe there was someone out there who would fit with her. Could there be? Was her own prince out there somewhere?

~~~

Princess Ava felt great relief that the interview was finally over. She hadn't realized how stressful it'd be to dodge the hard questions and spin fairy tale answers. She wanted their story to be the pinnacle of happily ever after. She wanted young girls to read her story with dreamy optimism, and her peers to read it with envy. The girls in her town had not been kind to her growing up. They'd looked down on her because of scandal and circumstance, but she was the one who'd ended up in the castle. She was the one the Prince had chosen out of all of them. And she wanted to remind them all.

She'd found herself speculating about Jill's life. She'd tried to draw her out, but Jill had always turned the conversation back to her. Jill seemed lonely and cynical and probably bitter, and Princess Ava had tried to give her hope. She was certainly
~~~

familiar with all of those feelings, but maybe her story would give Jill the courage to believe in her dreams again.

They'd had some long conversations, and she thought back, wondering if she'd revealed more than she'd intended. She was pretty confident it had gone well and couldn't wait to see the article. She'd feel better once her husband read it and would see that he'd given her a hard time for nothing.

Princess Ava joined the rest of the family in the smaller dining room for lunch. She could smell the warm rosemary rolls in a basket. Two huge vases of flowers adorned the table, and the polished wood reflected the deep red and violet hues. The King and Queen sat opposite each other at the long ends of the table, which made it difficult for them to hear each other. She and Prince Kellan sat opposite each other whenever he joined them, but most days he ate lunch at his desk.

She was pleased to see him sitting at the table today instead of sequestering himself in his office. Susan placed a small plate of salad in front of her as Sarah served the King and Queen.

"I finished the interview today," announced.

"Finally. How do you think it went?"

He helped himself to a warm roll and smeared butter on it. He used to offer one to her first.

"I think it went well," she answered.

"What happened to the well?" the King piped up.

"Nothing," Prince Kellan answered.

There was an enchanted wishing well on the property at the far end of the gardens. It was a small, circular well of rough-edged stones. The legend was that fairies had built it, and you could wish upon it, and if it pleased them, they would grant your wish.

Princess Ava remembered that she and the Prince had wished upon it on their wedding day. They had been married in the gardens because it was her favorite place. It reminded her of happy times with her mother. It was her haven.

"I hope you didn't tell her too much," Prince Kellan said as he turned his attention to his salad.

"I didn't tell her anything too personal."

"I still don't know why you agreed to it in the first place," he grumbled. "Nobody needs to know our business."

"I like to share our story. It's romantic. Don't you think so?"

"I suppose," he answered reluctantly.

"Kell, I really liked what you said in Dr. Tucker's office," she said. "It makes me remember how things used to be between us."

He loudly crunched some croutons.

"Where are the children?" Queen Aurora asked suddenly.

"They're in school," Prince Kellan answered loudly.

"You know, when you said you saw me with my mother for the first time sitting on a bench in the gardens," Princess Ava reminded him.

"Is Kell hiding in the gardens?" Queen Aurora asked.

"I'm right here, Mother," Prince Kellan said.

"What happened to the well?" King Kellan asked again.

"The fairies set it on fire," Prince Kellan mumbled.

Princess Ava giggled and covered her mouth with a napkin. Her husband glanced at her with an amused smile and shrugged.

~~~

Princess Ava was early for therapy. In fact, she'd gotten there before Prince Kellan. She was very proud of herself. He looked surprised when he came
~~~

in and sat down on the love seat beside her. Dr. Tucker entered and pulled over a chair to face them.

"It's good to see you both here on time." Dr. Tucker smiled at her and she beamed back. "I think we're getting to the heart of your issues, and I believe we can accomplish a great deal. So, first I'd like to ask if there's anything new you'd like to bring up."

"I finished the interview," Princess Ava offered.

"Good. Would either of you like to share how you feel about it?"

"I'm concerned about what the article will say," Prince Kellan admitted.

"I think it went fine," Princess Ava said.

"Okay. We'll talk about this more when the article comes out," Dr. Tucker said. "Did you both bring the lists that I asked you to work on last time?"

Prince Kellan held a piece of paper in his hand, and Princess Ava realized she'd left hers on her dresser. She hadn't worked on it much, anyway. Her answers were pretty obvious, and the whole exercise seemed silly.

"Do you need to go get your list?" Dr. Tucker asked her.

She shook her head. "I remember what's on it."

"All right, then. Who would like to share first?" he asked.

"You can go first," she told Prince Kellan. She was curious to hear what he had to say.

He looked at the paper in his hand for a moment. "I put a lot of thought into this because I think when we're young we don't think about what's important to us in a relationship and partner," he intoned. "I was lucky because my parents have a strong marriage and gave me lots of love and attention."

"That's a good point." Dr. Tucker nodded. "Ava, what kind of relationship did your parents have?"

"They had... They didn't have a relationship that I could see," she responded. "My mother was unhappy, and she left when I was a teenager."

"How did you feel about that?" Dr. Tucker probed.

"I didn't blame her. I felt sorry for my father, but I knew they weren't happy," she said. "I thought my mother would come back for me, but she never did, so I was stuck. It was a bummer."

The men glanced at each other before Prince Kellan continued.

"I always expected to have a relationship like my parents," he explained. "I wanted a partner who'd help me make the world a better place. I think it's important when you have a position of power to use it in a positive way. I wanted a partner who was generous and compassionate and sensitive to the needs of others. Someone who was well read and loved children and was honest and didn't care about all the perks and frills of life here in the castle."

"Get real."

Had she said that out loud? They both looked at Princess Ava. So, apparently, she had.

"I mean, you're talking about a saint. You're not talking about a real woman."

"I thought because you grew up struggling that you'd want to help others," Prince Kellan said. "But all you care about are superficial things."

"Ava," Dr. Tucker addressed her. "Why don't you share what you have on your list? What's important to you in a relationship and a partner?"

"Well, I think it's pretty obvious what's important in a relationship," she said. "I've always wanted romance and passion and adventure. I mean, I married a handsome Prince. Wouldn't you think it'd go without saying that that's the most romantic thing ever? It was wonderful between us in the beginning. We had an intense longing for each other, and I felt like I was all he wanted. I don't know what happened."

She looked down at her hands in her lap. She was sad about the loss of those feelings between them.

"It sounds like you have very different expectations about what your relationship should be like," Dr. Tucker noted. "Your childhoods and your parents' marriages have shaped who you are and what you want from a partner. At the beginning, you found a place to connect. You each need to think about where the other person is coming from, and then we'll find a place where you can meet again and reconnect."

Princess Ava sighed. She didn't see how they could do that. Her husband was more concerned with the rest of the world than with her. When had he turned his attention away from her? It had been so long ago, she couldn't remember.

She crossed her arms. They didn't understand her at all. No matter what she said, they twisted it around and made it sound ridiculous. It wasn't rocket science. She shouldn't have to spell it out for Kellan about how to be romantic.

She tried to think back and figure out at what point they had grown apart. Had it started with the children? Or was it his charitable work that had drawn his attention? Or had he just surmised that they were too different? He'd gotten pretty angry when she'd decorated their bedroom in pink and lace and flowery prints. Or was it because she'd stay up late reading her romance novels with the light on?

"Those stupid books have given you a warped sense of relationships," Prince Kellan complained. "They just feed this unrealistic romantic fantasy. How can any man live up to that, especially in a long marriage?"

"If you love someone, then it shouldn't be so hard to be romantic," she retorted. "I didn't know it was such an effort to feel romantic towards me."

"That's not what I meant, and you know it," he answered. "Marriages evolve. All that crazy, romantic stuff happens at the beginning."

"All you care about now are your charities," she accused. "You're too busy to pay any attention to me."

"What do you mean? We see each other every day," he protested.

She rolled her eyes. "We see each other at meals and in passing. Otherwise, you're always in your office, and you don't want me to interrupt you. I don't think you want to spend any time with me at all."

They both sat silently fuming.

Dr. Tucker looked from one to the other. "I can hear the frustration in your voices. You've each found an escape from intimacy. Kellan's escape is his work, and Ava's escape is reading her novels. It's easy to blame each other and not recognize your own participation."

They glanced at each other sullenly.

"It's very difficult," Dr. Tucker continued. "To break out of long-term patterns that feel safe. You'll feel resistance to this idea, so all I want you to do right now is think about it. I also want you to come up with little things you can do for the other person to make them happy. You can take little steps toward each other to break through these patterns. How does that sound?"

"I've done nothing wrong," Princess Ava objected.

"It's not about blaming each other," Prince Kellan said impatiently. He looked at Dr. Tucker. "She doesn't get it."

"It's going to be very difficult to let go of the anger and resentment that's built up over the years," Dr. Tucker emphasized. "I want you both to think of positive things to say to each other and little ways to make the other person happy. Try not to think of the other person as the enemy. We're all on the same side. It will take some effort to get out of the habit of reacting in your usual ways to each other. So, take a moment and put some thought into how you respond to each other and do things to make your partner happy. These small steps will be the beginning of finding your way back to each other."

"I agree," Prince Kellan said. "It makes sense."

Whatever, Princess Ava thought. Sometimes she felt like a prisoner in the castle with her crazy in-laws wandering about, and her husband hiding away in his office, and her children out in the world having fun. All she had were her books.

The truth was Princess Ava was lonely, even though it looked like she had everything anybody could want. How ironic that the reality of her lifelong dream was a twisted version of what she'd imagined. She'd agreed to therapy because her husband believed that all this talking and arguing would help. Here was the little thing she'd done for him. But what had he done for her lately?

Maybe she should have run away years ago when she'd had the chance.

16 Lost Lust

Princess Ava was sitting on a bench in the gardens sipping tea and eating a warm, poppy seed muffin. She had thrown a few cookies on the ground for the sprites. They favored the cookies. The sun was warm, and a slight breeze ruffled the flowers and stirred up a wonderful scent.

She liked to start her day this way when the weather was nice. The castle was so old and dark and musty that it often felt claustrophobic to her. Plus, her in-laws were constantly underfoot, and it was impossible to have a conversation with them anymore, which was just as well since she'd always sensed that they hadn't approved of the marriage. She felt she'd been a disappointment to them, despite giving them three grandchildren who were the joys of their lives.

There had been more suitable women the Prince could've married, those who would've shared his desire to help the world. She'd spent her entire childhood working to please other people. All she wanted was freedom and an easy, leisurely life. She'd earned it.

But now it was a requirement of therapy to think of ways to please her husband. She knew exactly what would please him. What pleases any man? But it wouldn't be like it was in her books. Some passages in the books would make her burn with desire, but it had been so long and she didn't want to mess up her bed. Prince Kellan's room was too dark and not at all romantic. Besides, he had no clue how to seduce her and get her in the mood. He should know how to do that by now. It was his own fault.

She saw a pure white peacock cross the path, heading toward the roses. She quietly got up to follow it. She loved the peacocks. They seemed appropriately regal.

"Good morning." Prince Kellan had come outside.

She was surprised to see him. She frowned at him and sat back down. He sat beside her.

"I forgot how nice it is out here. It smells wonderful, and the sun is warm. I can see why you like to sit out here." He glanced around. "Did you see that white peacock over there?"

"Yeah." It was all she could think to say.

"I know it's nice to get away from my parents," he commented. "They can be hard to manage, and you deal with them more than I do."

"They usually don't find me out here," she admitted. She wondered why he'd come outside. What did he want?

They sat silently for a few moments. It felt awkward. She pulled her book closer to her leg and tried to cover it with her dress, but she drew his attention.

"What are you reading?" he asked.

She sighed and held up the book, waiting for his disparaging remarks.

"'*Love's Forbidden Passion Series: Book 5.*'" He read on the cover. "'*Lust in the Dust.*'" He looked at her with an amused grin before he turned the book over and read the description aloud. "'Danielle has led a sheltered life and never ventured far from home. But when her mother's plane crashes in the desert under mysterious circumstances, she must travel to this barren place to find her. If she's still alive. Can she trust Derek, who had been seated next to her mother on the plane, or is he hiding the truth? Find out in this sizzling romance and feel the heat.'"

Prince Kellan raised his eyebrows as he handed the book back to her. "Seriously?"

"I know it's silly," she said. "But it's fun to read."

He shrugged. "Actually, it does sound fun to read."

"You think so?"

"Yeah. Let's see." He took it back, opened it to a random page, and read out loud. "'She had never met anyone like Derek. He seemed to know her thoughts. She blushed and looked down, but then she couldn't help looking back up into his intense gaze and dark good looks. He smiled at her, revealing perfect white teeth. Then he turned and grabbed the shovel and continued digging. The afternoon sun was scorching, and he took his shirt off and wiped his brow. She watched the sweat drip down his bare stomach and noticed his rippling muscles. She longed to run her fingers over his shoulders and back. But no! She mustn't think this way. She had to find her mother.'" Prince Kellan was laughing, and she couldn't help laughing with him.

"It's a guilty pleasure." She shrugged.

He handed the book back to her. "So is that what you like? Perfect white teeth and rippling muscles?"

Princess Ava couldn't keep from blushing. "Lots of women like these books," she said defensively.

"Obviously," he answered. "This is the fifth book in the series. Have you read the ones before it?"

"A few." *All* of them.

He shook his head and looked around at the flowers that bobbed in the breeze. She wondered how long he'd sit there before he fled back to his office. But he turned to her and took her hand.

"I do love you, you know. I guess, in a lot of ways, we don't understand each other." He sighed. "I just want us to be close again. But I don't think I can live up to the sexy, perfect men in your books."

"I never expected you to," she assured him.

"I hope not." He grinned. "Do you want me to go get a shovel and dig up the gardens?"

She smiled. "I don't think that's necessary."

"Good. I don't know if my sweat would be as appealing." He chuckled.

They sat silently for a few moments. A subtle

fragrance wafted around them. The well they'd wished on those many years ago came into Princess Ava's thoughts. It was way back in a far corner of the gardens. She wasn't sure she could even find it.

"I'm glad we're working on our relationship," Prince Kellan said. "I don't know how you feel about Dr. Tucker, but I think he's pretty insightful. I feel optimistic about us. I hope you do too."

"I guess so," she said.

"Do you think it was a mistake to get married so fast?" he asked. "Maybe we should've gotten to know each other better. Things happened pretty quickly between us."

"Yes, they did." She wasn't sure what he wanted her to say. Was he looking for reassurance that they'd done the right thing? "We were in love."

"I hope we still are, Ava." Prince Kellan squeezed her hand.

~~~

Princess Ava smoothed the wrinkles from the skirt of her dress. It was a light lilac color with faded white and pink flowers. The design was so delicate, you could only see the flowers if you looked closely at the pattern. It had taken a long time to find shoes that were the same lilac color. She would've had shoes made, but her husband seemed irritated when she did things like that. He just didn't understand how important appearances were.

"Ava, if you're ready," Dr. Tucker said.

He and Prince Kellan were both looking at her.

"Of course. What was the question?" she blurted.

Her husband shook his head and sighed. What was his problem? She was here, wasn't she? These sessions were dull and tiresome. They should do something more fun together, though nothing they'd both enjoy came to mind.
~~~

"Do you have anything to say since our last meeting?" Dr. Tucker asked patiently.

"It was nice when you came out and talked to me in the gardens the other day," she said politely to Prince Kellan to show them she was cooperating with therapy.

"Yes, it was," he agreed. "I know you love the gardens, so we should take walks in the evening like we used to."

"That sounds nice."

They would stroll through the gardens at dusk, holding hands. The fountains would mist them as they passed, while the peacocks wandered amongst the plants and flowers. Sometimes the sprites would knock something over and startle them, and it would make them laugh. She missed those times. She wished they could recapture the romance of being newlyweds.

"Good," Dr. Tucker said. "Ava, have you thought about anything you could do for your husband that would make him happy?"

She felt herself blushing.

"It's those books," Prince Kellan explained to Dr. Tucker. "She can't get her mind out of those books. I think they've warped her view of reality."

"Nah, uh. I know they're just stories, and I know they're kind of trivial, but I enjoy them."

"Let's get back on track," Dr. Tucker suggested.

"Kellan would like me to help him with his work," Princess Ava answered reluctantly because she couldn't think of anything else, and she hadn't given it much thought.

"Would you?" he asked eagerly. "It would be a great help. There's so much to do before the conference."

Conference? She couldn't remember him talking about a conference, but she didn't want to admit it.

"When is it?"

"We have a few weeks."

"Okay. I can help you."

Darn! Now she'd have to follow through. She found his work incredibly boring. He was always on his computer reading articles and looking at statistics or composing documents or talking on the phone. It all seemed so tedious and unexciting. Why would anyone voluntarily do this? It was like being in school and doing homework.

"Very good." This pleased Dr. Tucker. "These are positive steps. You'll be spending more time together in a way that makes each of you happy."

Princess Ava stifled a yawn. Thankfully, they were wrapping things up. Prince Kellan would be elated that they were winning Dr. Tucker's approval. He always wanted to do the right thing.

He followed her as they left Dr. Tucker's office. He usually went his own way. What did he want? Did he expect her to help in his office right away? She turned to face him and he grinned.

"Come on." He took her hand and pulled her with him.

"Where are we going?" she asked.

The last thing she wanted to do was head over to his office. Why had she opened her big mouth? But instead, he led her into their private wing and right up to her bedroom door.

"What are you doing?" she asked with confusion.

"I don't have a shovel," he said with a mischievous smile. "Or rippling muscles."

He pulled her to him and kissed her deeply. She relaxed against him and warmth spread through her body. Then he reached back and pushed open her bedroom door.

"Kell! It's the middle of the day," she complained despite her racing heart.

"Better than the middle of the desert." He grinned and pulled at her dress. "How do you get this thing off? There's so much material. Are you under there somewhere?"

"Be careful," she warned. "This is an expensive dress. It's very delicate. You're going to rip it."

"I won't rip it," he said with exasperation. He pulled his shoes off.

Princess Ava stared at her neat ruffled bed. Her lace pillows were arranged so perfectly. This pink room could be featured in a magazine as the epitome of romance. She should've had Jill take a picture of it for her magazine. Why hadn't she thought of that?

"This is exactly what we need," Prince Kellan told her. "We just need to be close again." He unzipped his pants and then came over to her and spun her around. "Isn't there a zipper or something? Does this just go over your head?" He fumbled with the layered skirts.

"You can't just pull it off me," she cried. "It's very delicate."

"It must take you an hour to put this thing on," he said. "Just get it off."

"Very romantic," she said sarcastically. "Is this supposed to get me in the mood?"

"Sorry I'm not one of the perfect guys in your books," he responded.

Then he noticed her bookshelf. He approached it and snatched a book.

"'*Love's Forbidden Passion Series: Book 3*,'" he read. "'*Lust at Sea*.'" He threw it down on the floor. "I can't believe you read this crap. Is this what you need to get in the mood? Just let it go. Just let it be you and me right now. Can't you do that?"

Princess Ava stood there frozen. Then she went over and gingerly picked up the book. She placed it back on the bookshelf. She didn't know what to say to him.

17 The Wishing Well

"Wake up, sleepyhead," Kent whispered.

Ava opened her eyes to see him standing over her wearing his baseball cap. She was groggy and struggled to sit up. He kneeled down beside her and held out a canteen.

"Here. Drink some water."

"I have to go to the bathroom," she said.

"Okay. I have some toilet paper." He dug around in his backpack and pulled out a roll.

"I have to go in the woods?" she asked, appalled. "I can't do that."

"I don't see any restrooms around," he reasoned.

She took the toilet paper and got up.

"This is just temporary," he said.

Oh, my gosh. This was getting worse and worse. She had to add plumbing to her list of necessities that currently included a warm bed located indoors.

"Drink some water," he said when she returned.

She drank the cool water out of the canteen and handed it back to him. He put it in his backpack along with the toilet paper.

"I want to talk to you," he said solemnly.

Ava sat down on the sleeping bag and yawned. She was hardly awake and tried to ignore her grumbling stomach.

"It's okay if you've changed your mind. I want you to know that you can change your mind at any time and go back. I know things are rough right now, but I swear to you they'll get better." He took both her hands and looked into her eyes. "I promise you."

"Okay," she said timidly.

She wanted so much to believe him, but she wasn't thrilled with their present situation.

He released her hands, leaned over, and kissed her slowly. His lips were soft and warm, and she felt herself melt a little. It strengthened her resolve to stick with him.

He pulled back and stared into her eyes. "I think I love you," he said softly. "I really do. I never stop thinking about you. I don't know what it is, but I feel like we belong together. Do you feel that too?"

Ava looked at his earnest face in the early morning light. She'd mostly seen him in darkened rooms. Light freckles were sprinkled across his nose. She felt affection for those freckles.

"Yes." She nodded. Then she said something she never thought she'd say. "I don't care about living in the castle. I've dreamed about it my entire life, and that's what I thought I was meant to do. Then I met you, and I feel the same way you do. I just want to be with you, even if things are rough at first. I don't care." She brushed aside her worries.

Kent sat back with a big smile on his face. "What a relief to hear you say that. I needed to hear it. I just had to know that it was me you wanted and not... not what I could give you."

What did he mean by that? He had nothing to give her. Sometimes things went over her head, but it didn't matter. They were together, and he would take care of her. She leaned over and drew him into a kiss again. She couldn't get enough of him.

Suddenly, she heard rustling, and her eyes widened. She hoped Kent would protect her from whatever animal was about to emerge to attack them. It sounded like something big breaking through the branches. Their adventure hadn't lasted very long, but at least they'd die together.

Ava heard laughter. Agnes was standing there shaking some bushes.

"Geez. Come up for air, will you?" she remarked. "You should've seen your face." She bent over laughing.

"Agnes, what are you doing here?" Ava blurted.

Agnes stepped into the clearing. "So, this is your

little love nest. I like what you've done with the place."

"How did you find us?" Ava asked.

"I have my ways." Agnes put her hands on her hips. "This is the guy, huh? This is the one you couldn't shut up about?"

Ava glanced at Kent. "Yes. We're in love, and we're running away, so get used to it," she answered defiantly.

"Do you know how old this girl is?" Agnes glared at Kent, who seemed to be examining the ground. "I'll tell you. She's underage. I can have you arrested."

"Stop it, Agnes," Ava said firmly. "I'll be eighteen in just a few months. You can't stop me."

"Well, aren't you going to introduce us?" Agnes asked testily.

"Kent, this is my fairy godmother, Agnes," she said. "Agnes, this is my boyfriend, Kent." She liked the sound of that.

"Charmed. I'm sure." Agnes held out her hand, and he stood and quickly shook it.

"Hey." Agnes hung onto his hand and tried to peek under the visor of his cap. "You look familiar. Wait a minute. I know who you are."

Kent pulled his hand away and kept his head lowered.

"You don't know, do you?" she said to Ava.

"Know what? You know Kent?"

"Lots of people know Kent," Agnes answered with a big smile.

"Did you go to the high school?" Ava asked him.

She tried to recall if she'd ever seen him around. He looked a little familiar now that Agnes had mentioned it. But where had she seen him?

"No. I didn't go to the high school." He glowered at Agnes. "Don't say anything. I mean it."

Agnes looked amused. She made a gesture as if locking her lips.

"Carry on, kids." She walked away chuckling.

Ava turned to Kent. "How do you know Agnes?"

"My parents know her," he answered tersely.

"Is she your fairy godmother too?" she wondered.

"Not a chance," he said emphatically. "No offense, but she's a mess."

"She's doing better," Ava said in her defense. "You may not like her, but she's the only one who believed in me. She's the only one who cared about me at all." She was getting emotional and tears threatened.

"I'm sorry." Kent wrapped his arms around her. "Don't worry. Now you have me, and I'll take care of you. All of our dreams will come true as long as we're together. I promise this to you, Ava."

~~~

Ava was so hungry she couldn't stand it. They had walked a long way, and she had no clue where they were. They could've gone in circles for all she knew. Kent was eager to keep going, but he'd promised that they'd stop once they came upon a place to eat.

"Do you think your father or Hazel will report that you're missing?" he asked as they trudged on.

"I doubt it. They're already in trouble for keeping me out of school."

"Do you miss going to school?"

"Not really. I didn't have many friends. It was humiliating when my mother took off, and everyone was talking about it, so it was kind of a relief to be out of there," she said. "Besides, it was hard to stay awake in class."

"I didn't get to go to school either," he shared. "It was pretty lonely. I always thought it'd be fun to be in school with the other kids."

"You weren't missing anything." Her stomach
~~~

growled loudly. "I'm starving."

They came upon a small strip of stores along the road. A gas station was at one end, and a small old-fashioned diner was tucked at the other end. Ava was extremely relieved. They went inside and found a booth, setting their backpacks next to them.

"There's not much that's good on here." Kent squinted at the menu.

Everything sounded good to Ava. She ordered a grilled cheese sandwich and fries. He ordered soup and salad and helped himself to some of her fries. She felt much better with food in her stomach.

"Didn't you say we were going to get a car today?" she asked, dipping a French fry in ketchup.

"That's the plan," he replied. "Are you sure that you're sure about all this?"

"Well, I sure want a car," she answered with a smile. "Once we get a car and our own place, things will be great. I know you'll figure everything out. Why? Are you worried?"

He nodded. "I have to figure out how to get the car."

"What do you mean?" she asked, wiping up a drop of ketchup on the table with her napkin.

"It's at my parents'. I think I can get it without them seeing us."

"Your parents?" She pondered this a moment. "Is it your car?"

"It's complicated," Kent answered with a sigh. "I don't want them to see me. They won't want me to leave again."

Ava was eyeing a small display case on the counter. "Can I have a chocolate donut?"

They sat on a picnic bench in the public park across the street as she finished the last of her donut. He was reluctant to go home, even to get the car. She watched some kids on the swing set as a couple passed by with a dog on a leash.

"The thing is that it will complicate things if I try to get the car," Kent explained. "I'll feel guilty and they'll want us to stay, and then we won't get to do all the things we want."

"Do they have a nice house?"

He looked over at her. "Why?"

"I wouldn't mind sleeping in a real bed and having a bathroom," she said hesitantly. "As long as we're together. Isn't that what matters?"

"Yes, but I don't want other people to tell us what we have to do." He seemed frustrated.

"What I really wish," she said, "is that we could just find a little cabin somewhere and that everybody would just leave us alone."

Kent nodded. "That's it exactly. You *do* understand."

"Where would we go if we had a car?"

"Anywhere we want," he said with a smile. "Anywhere the road takes us until we find a place we don't want to leave."

They sat lost in their separate musings. Ava would rather sleep inside on a warm bed that night. She hoped he'd decide to take her home with him. It couldn't be that bad. She was sure his family would be nicer than hers. Maybe they could get there in time for dinner.

"I have an idea," Kent said. "I think it will ensure our future together."

"What?"

"Do you believe in magic?" he asked her.

"Of course," she answered emphatically.

Finally, someone who didn't think it was crazy.

"There's a wishing well in the royal gardens," he said. "If we can get in, we can make a wish together."

"If we can get in," she repeated doubtfully.

He took her hands. "It will bind us together," he said earnestly. "We'll be making a commitment to each other."

She could see the sincerity in his eyes. She trusted him. She wanted to believe in their future together. She wanted so much to believe.

“Let’s do it,” he urged.

“Okay.” She beamed at him.

They put their backpacks on and trudged in the castle's direction. It had taken them so long to get this far away, and now they were circling back along the perimeter of town. How exasperating. But she was intrigued by this idea. She wanted to see this magical wishing well. She’d been in the royal gardens many times but had never seen it nor heard of it. She hoped they could find it, though she preferred not to go anywhere near the castle. It reminded her of lost dreams. Too many fervent dreams dreamed in vain. Yet something always drew her back, and a small part of her still wished for it.

Kent was dashing through the woods with familiarity, and she hurried to keep up. She contemplated what she’d wish for. She wanted Kent, and she wanted their own place, and she didn’t want to worry about having enough food or enough money. It wasn’t much to ask for, but seemed so out of reach. She fretted about what their future held. Where would they be a week from now? A month? A year?

It had gradually grown darker, and he pointed a flashlight to light their way. It was late by the time they reached the back edge of the castle. The night was velvety black, and the moon hid behind dark clouds. A wrought-iron fence encircled the vast property.

“How are we going to get in?” she asked as he drank water from the canteen.

He handed it to her. “I heard there’s a back gate that the gardeners use.”

“It’s probably locked,” she assumed, but he was already running along the fence.

Ava was having her doubts about this dubious plan. First, there was no way they were going to get in. And if they managed that, how would they find the well? The gardens were huge. There must be more than one well in there. How would they know which one was the magical one? They might just find an ordinary well. And what would happen if they got caught sneaking around the gardens at night?

She ran behind him as quickly as she could with her backpack bouncing awkwardly on her back. All she wanted to do was eat and sleep.

"I found it," Kent called to her in a loud whisper.

Ava caught up to him and sure enough, there was a gate.

"How do we get in?" she whispered.

He pushed on the latch, and it swung open. He beamed at her.

"That was easy," she marveled.

"Come on."

He entered, and she followed. It would be easy to get confused in the maze of pathways. They could end up wandering for days.

Ava grabbed Kent's arm. "We're going to get lost," she warned.

"No, we won't. I have a good sense of direction." He darted ahead of her.

How had she gotten herself into this mess? She followed him, turning onto paths left and right, back and forth, trying to remember which way they'd come. It was hopeless. They were lost.

They came across a circular clearing with curved stone benches, and she sat down. She took off her backpack. He noticed she wasn't behind him and came back. He handed her the canteen. The castle loomed into the sky, and the long windows spilled light. She'd never seen the castle this close up in the dark. She wondered what it was like inside. There were probably the softest beds and the plushest rugs. How she longed to lay her head on a pillow and snuggle under a warm comforter. She yawned.

"I know you're tired," Kent said. "We just need to find the well."

"I'm tired and I'm hungry and I'm cold," she whined. "We're never going to find that stupid well, and we're never going to find our way out of here."

Kent put his arm around her and hugged her. "I'll take care of you. I promise, Ava. Please trust me. I know I can find the well, and I promise everything will be all right. It may seem irrational, but I believe in the well's magic. I've heard stories my entire life about it. It means something to me."

She sat sullenly.

"I'm happy you're with me because you want to be," he said. "It just means so much. I can't... I don't trust many people. Most people want something from me, but I know you're not like that. I know you're different."

"Let's just find the well," she suggested wearily.

She stood and pulled her backpack onto her shoulders. Then she followed him and the beam of his flashlight along the path.

Kent had stopped. Had he finally accepted that they were lost? She caught up with him.

"What's wrong?" She felt a few drops of rain.

He pointed the flashlight, and she followed the light with her eyes. A small circular stone well was revealed in the shadows. It didn't look very impressive.

"How do we know that's the one?" she asked.

He moved the flashlight back and forth over it. The light caught sparkly specks floating beneath the bucket that hung over the opening. Bits of colored lights twinkled between the stones.

"This is it," Ava said with awe. "It's enchanted."

"Fairies live in the well. They decide whose wishes are granted," he murmured.

"We should've brought them something," she said. "But I don't know what fairies like."

Kent dropped the flashlight onto the soft mossy ground and took her hand.

"Put your other hand on the well," he instructed, and they both touched the well. "Now close your eyes and picture what you want in as much detail as possible."

Ava shut her eyes and imagined all the things she wanted. She wanted to live happily ever after with Kent. She wanted a family who loved her. She wanted to live in a beautiful place surrounded by beautiful things. She wanted cheerful flowers and rainbows stretched across the sky. And she never wanted to clean another room or make another bed.

More raindrops fell upon them. He pulled her into his arms, and they stood there holding each other while the rain fell harder. She looked around for cover. There was none. There was nothing to protect them. They only had each other.

"I love you, Kent," she said, overwhelmed with emotion as she blinked in the rain.

"I love you, Ava," he answered in the darkness, hugging her tightly.

Then he let her go as he bent over to pick up the flashlight.

"Who's out there?" a male voice yelled.

A beam of light was coming toward them. A man waved to them to follow. They'd been caught. Rain dripped off the visor of Kent's hat as they traipsed behind the man along the pathways to a side door of the castle. Kent held her hand as she trembled uncontrollably. She wasn't sure if it was from the cold or fear. What was the punishment for trespassing at the castle?

As soon as they entered the welcome warmth of an alcove, Kent said to the man, "Can I speak to you privately?" His head was down, and the rain dripped off his visor onto the floor.

The man was tall and thin and solemn. They stepped through a doorway, leaving her alone. She slipped off her wet backpack and stood there waiting and shivering.

After a few minutes, a matronly looking woman rushed toward her from another doorway.

"Oh, look at you. You're soaking wet. You poor thing. Let's get you some dry clothing. Come with me."

Ava slung her backpack over one shoulder and followed the woman. What had become of Kent? Had he taken all the blame? Would they have to pay a fine? Would they be thrown in jail? She hurried behind the spry woman down long hallway after long hallway and up some stairs and finally into a cozy bedroom. This was unexpected. Did they want her to clean rooms to atone for trespassing?

"There's a bathroom if you want to take a shower, and there should be some nightgowns and clean clothing to wear in the armoire," the woman said. "You must be tired. I'll come and get you for breakfast."

"Breakfast? Am I allowed to sleep here?" Ava asked with surprise.

Spend the night at the castle? Who knew they were so hospitable to trespassers? Perhaps they were waiting until morning to turn them in.

"Of course. I'll come for you in the morning."

"Wait. Do you know what happened to my friend?" Ava asked nervously.

"Oh." The woman looked perplexed. Then she smiled warmly. "He's just fine. You'll see him tomorrow. Get some sleep." She turned to leave and then turned back. "How rude of me. I didn't tell you my name. I'm Cora."

"I'm Ava. I'm so sorry we were trespassing. I hope we're not in trouble."

"Of course not," Cora assured her. "Just get some sleep. It's late."

Ava took a long, hot shower and hung her clothes to dry in the bathroom. She found a flannel nightgown in the armoire that was a size too large and crawled into the most comfortable bed she'd ever lain upon, falling instantly asleep.

18 The Royal Charitable Trust

Prince Kellan snored suddenly, waking Princess Ava. The comforter was on the floor, and her pastel pink sheets were tangled around them. Had it really happened? She couldn't remember the last time. She felt wiped out. The sheets were damp with sweat. She must be a mess. What time was it? It was still light out. She was surprised she'd fallen asleep in the middle of the day. She was even more surprised at what had happened in the middle of the day.

She looked over at her husband. He was sprawled on her bed with his mouth slightly open. He was just so clueless about romance. How ironic that such a handsome Prince, who was the epitome of every girl's fantasies, didn't know how to be romantic. Had he always been like that, or had the books warped her expectations like he kept accusing?

A knock on the door startled her.

"Yes? What is it?" she called out.

Prince Kellan lifted his head. "What's wrong?"

"You have a visitor, Princess," Sarah announced through the door.

"Thank you. I'll be there in a few minutes," she called back. She looked around. The room was in disarray, and she sighed. "I'm taking a shower. You can take one after me unless you want to sleep more," she told Prince Kellan.

He had already fallen back asleep.

Princess Ava wondered who was waiting for her. It could be anybody. People from the past would frequently show up at the castle soliciting her help. It was so bothersome. The last thing she wanted to do was help someone who hadn't been civil to her or had ignored her. Thankfully, it didn't happen so much anymore. She was hoping it would be Jill with a copy of the article. She couldn't wait to read it.

Prince Kellan was absent from her room by the time she got out of the shower. She was glad because she wanted some privacy to dress and fix herself up. The room was still a big mess, and she shook her head at the sight of it. Oh well. Maybe he'd be happy with her for a while now. It hadn't been as romantic as it was in her books, but it had been quite pleasurable, actually.

Princess Ava went down to the main sitting room. It was where the staff brought guests to wait. Sunlight still spilled past the heavy drapes onto the plush rug. She didn't know what time it was, but her stomach told her it must be close to dinnertime. She certainly felt famished.

Agnes stood looking out the window. They saw each other now and then. Her hair had turned completely gray, but she was still as feisty as ever.

"Hey, kid." Agnes turned as she came in. "You look fantastic. You're glowing. Don't tell me you're pregnant again?" She let out a guffaw. "Nah. Being married to that handsome Prince still agrees with you."

"Hello, Agnes," she said with reticence. Agnes never showed up unless she wanted something. "How are you? I thought you retired. Didn't you move into a retirement community?"

"Yeah. It's pretty boring," she answered. "Do you have any of those pastries handy?"

"I'm sure they'll bring something in for us," Princess Ava assured her.

She sat on one of the floral couches, and Agnes perched opposite her.

"So," Agnes said. "I've come for your firstborn. Or is it your last born? I can't remember now. Which one am I supposed to get?"

"What?" Princess Ava frowned.

Susan briskly entered carrying a tray with tea and pastries. She set it down on the coffee table between them.

"Thank you, Susan," Princess Ava said.

Susan nodded her head and retreated.

"You don't know how I crave these things." Agnes snatched a pastry off the tray. "You can't find these anywhere. They're so flaky and delicious. It's going to make my stomach hurt, but it'll be worth it."

"Agnes, what are you talking about? Firstborn. Last born. The kids are almost grown up. This is ridiculous."

Agnes chuckled. "I can always get you. I'm kidding. What would I do with a kid?"

"Well, then. Why are you here?"

"What? I can't visit an old friend?" Agnes responded indignantly.

"Fine. Whatever." Princess Ava reached for a pastry.

"I just thought you'd want to know that I talked to that journalist. She tracked me down somehow."

"You talked to Jill?" A feeling of panic rose within the Princess. "What did she ask you? What did you say to her?"

"Relax," Agnes said. "I was discreet. Give me some credit."

"But what if our stories contradict each other?" Princess Ava moaned. "This isn't good."

"What did you do? Make up a bunch of stuff?" Agnes asked, chewing.

"Not really. Maybe a little. I just made things sound... nicer."

"I hate to be the bearer of bad news, but the real reason I came here to talk to you is because the spell has an expiration date," Agnes informed her. "You'd think they last forever, but what are you going to do?"

"What spell?"

"What do you mean, what spell? How do you think the Prince fell madly in love with you?" Agnes asked. "You may have noticed it wearing off a little by now."

"I thought you couldn't make somebody fall in love," Princess Ava protested.

"It's all semantics, you know. Maybe love is the wrong word. He's been blinded to your deficiencies, but then I guess love is blind, anyway. So maybe he really loves you. We'll soon find out." Agnes finished off her pastry.

"The royals don't believe in divorce," Princess Ava stated.

"Lucky for you," Agnes said.

"We've been married almost 25 years," Princess Ava told her.

Had it all been because of a spell? She couldn't believe that. She didn't want to lose her Prince. Not because he was a prince, but because she really loved Kellan. She had always loved him, even before they'd technically met.

~~~

"This afternoon was wonderful, darling." Prince Kellan came over and kissed the top of her head after dinner. "Let's take a walk in the gardens."

She took his extended hand, and he led her outside. The air had cooled, and soon the solar lanterns would light the pathways.

"Are you warm enough?" he asked.

She nodded. "Yes."

"I didn't want to lose this great feeling I have about us," he said as they meandered, holding hands. "Do you remember when we used to do this every evening after dinner?"

"Yes. It's nice."

Her head was filled with uneasy thoughts. She didn't want her husband to stop loving her. Was it all because of a spell? But Agnes wasn't that powerful,
~~~

was she? Would this loving feeling dissipate? She didn't want her entire world to come crashing down. Prince Kellan would certainly never divorce her, but they'd been living separate lives for a long time. Maybe years. When had this happened? Why had it happened? Did it matter as long as she was still living in this beautiful castle with her beautiful clothes and these beautiful gardens?

"Why are you so quiet?" he asked her. "What are you thinking about?"

"Nothing."

Prince Kellan stopped and turned to face her. "I want you to be happy. I want us to be happy together."

"I want that too," she said, and realized she meant it with all her heart. It wasn't enough to just live here. She wanted it all. Love and luxury with her Prince.

"Do you remember what we did on our wedding night?" he asked.

Princess Ava looked down and blushed. "Of course I do."

"No, not that." He laughed. "Come on."

He pulled her along the pathway, past rows and rows of flowers and lush foliage. He hurried her along a maze of crisscrossing paths. He was heading towards the far corner of the gardens.

And then she saw it. It stood half hidden, tucked in a corner by the high wrought-iron fence that bordered the property. The old stone well was decrepit and crumbling with ivy curling and twisting around it. It was smaller than she remembered. The little roof covering it was layered with moss. She hadn't seen the well in years.

Prince Kellan spoke. "We made a wish together that night. I think this old wishing well still holds some magic. If we make the same wish again, we can live happily together for another 25 years."

It was dusk. The sun was sinking in the sky. The lanterns were giving off a soft glow. This moment seemed perfect. She put her arms around him and leaned her head on his shoulder.

"I don't think it can give me anything I don't already have." Princess Ava sighed happily.

Then it occurred to her that this could be the magic spell Agnes had cited that was about to expire.

"But it couldn't hurt," she said, lifting her head.

Princess Ava took Prince Kellan's hand, and they stepped toward the well as they had decades ago on that rainy night.

~~~

Dr. Tucker was delighted. "I'd like to commend you both for making so much progress. I can see by looking at you you're both happier and more connected."

"We've had some good quality time together," Prince Kellan told him. "Haven't we, darling?" He squeezed Princess Ava's hand.

"Yes, we have," she agreed.

She hoped they could stop therapy now. She'd never felt comfortable airing their personal issues with Dr. Tucker. He was a man. Of course, he'd better understand her husband and take his side.

"Just because you've leaped ahead in your progress doesn't mean that you can stop your efforts now. It's more important than ever to continue this forward momentum," Dr. Tucker advised. "Now let's get into a little more detail about these positive changes. What sort of activities did you do together that strengthened your bond?"

Princess Ava could feel herself blushing, and she stared down at her lap.

Prince Kellan chuckled. "My wife gets embarrassed, but we were able to be intimate. It's
~~~

been a long time since we've been physical, and it felt very good to be that close again."

"What do you think has gotten in the way of this happening more often?" Dr. Tucker pursued.

"Well." Prince Kellan looked at her. "I don't know. I think walls of misunderstanding and anger built up between us. It made us feel very separate, but I just broke through because I didn't want to give up."

"You blamed my books," she reminded him.

"That too," he acknowledged. "I felt I couldn't live up to this romantic ideal that she has from these books. It's unrealistic that she expects me to emulate these men." He shook his head. "I just worked on getting past my insecurity and can see now how silly it was to compete with these fictional characters. I mean, those books are pretty ridiculous."

"What are you thinking, Ava?" Dr. Tucker addressed her.

She looked up. "I guess some of them are a little silly, but I like them. They make me believe in romance and passion."

"We have romance and passion," Prince Kellan said defensively.

"I don't think we have a lot of romance," she said. "If you want me to be honest." He'd asked for it.

"Okay," Dr. Tucker said. "It sounds like your wife wants a little more romance. You may not agree, but this is not about you. This is about doing something a little extra that will make your wife happy. Just think about it."

"Okay." Prince Kellan had let go of her hand and looked a little deflated.

"What else did you to do together that was bonding?" Dr. Tucker addressed Princess Ava.

"We've been taking walks in the gardens like we used to when we were first married," she answered. "It's nice."

"Good. Good." He nodded. "You mentioned last

time that you'd be helping your husband with his work. How is that going?"

"Uh." Princess Ava glanced guiltily at Prince Kellan. "I haven't had time, but I promise I will." She looked at him. "I'll help you later or tomorrow. Just let me know what you want me to do. I want to help you."

"The conference has been postponed, so we have more time now," he informed her. "But I'd still appreciate your help."

"You got it," she said, and this time she meant it.

~~~

Princess Ava squinted at the computer. She was entering numbers from a document into a spreadsheet. Prince Kellan was on the phone with the Danish Ambassador again. She wished he'd just hire an assistant, but she knew he wanted her to help him. It was important to him that she was involved with his work.

These were definitely some pretty interesting statistics about world population. Apparently, overpopulation was a big issue in many countries, creating cascading problems of poverty and shortages of resources. She didn't know how these problems could be solved. For some reason, her husband cared about these issues in other countries and believed that he had a responsibility to do something. It was admirable, despite the futility of such ambitious endeavors.

And it didn't stop there. He was also a big proponent of alternative energies. He was constantly droning on about wind power and solar power and geothermal technologies. He talked about new advances with lithium batteries and hybrid vehicles. She tried to pay attention, but most of the time it just made her sleepy. She was getting very good at
~~~

smiling and nodding and stifling yawns.

"I'm so glad you're helping me." Prince Kellan was off the phone. "Pretty interesting stuff, huh?" He looked over her shoulder.

"Fascinating," she answered.

"This is how I always pictured things. The two of us working together to make the world a better place. We're really making a difference with the money in the trust."

"The trust?" Princess Ava wasn't sure what he was talking about.

"Your jewelry originally funded the Royal Charitable Trust, and it's enabled us to get involved in several important projects. I'm very excited about the wells. Many people around the world don't have access to clean water. Can you imagine that? It's such a basic need, yet some people have to walk miles a day just for clean water."

"Miles?" she repeated. That couldn't be true. He must be exaggerating.

He sat down at his desk. "I hope eventually the children will become involved. They need to be aware of what's going on in the world and how important it is to do something when you're in a position like we are."

"They're young," she commented.

"I know." He swiveled his chair back and forth with a thoughtful look on his face. "I hope we haven't spoiled them too much. The problem is that they're too insulated from the real world. I think we should have them come home this summer."

"They're already coming home for our anniversary party," she reminded him.

"I think they should stay home instead of partying in Monaco or wherever everyone is partying this year," he said with a frown.

"They're not going to like that," Princess Ava mumbled.

"I want to spend some time with them and educate them about the trust and the work that we're doing," he continued with fervor. "The more I think about it, the more I realize we haven't done a very good job educating them about the world and our responsibilities as royals."

She nodded supportively.

"I think I'm going to take them with me to some of these countries, so they can see the devastating conditions that people live in and how important our work is. We have the opportunity to improve so many lives."

"Good idea," she said.

Her husband had a good heart, and she pictured him as a hero saving the world. Now that was a nice image.

"We still have to plan the party," she reminded him.

Prince Kellan smiled warmly at her. "Our twenty-fifth anniversary."

"Yes." She smiled.

A party. Now this was something she could get excited about.

"We never really had a honeymoon," he said. "You wanted to settle in here, which is understandable. It was quite an adjustment for you, but you always wanted to travel, and we never really got a chance to, other than trips related to royal obligations."

"I'm not complaining," she assured him.

"I know." He was still smiling at her.

"What?" Why was he grinning at her like that?

"I have a surprise for you for our anniversary."

Princess Ava perked up. "What is it?" Jewelry, perhaps? It had been a while since she'd gotten new jewelry.

"We're taking a trip to Europe," he announced. "I was going to wait to tell you, but I can't. I owe it to you. We'll travel all around Europe and stay at the most extravagant places. They love hosting royals. We can see all the museums and tourist sites and do some shopping."

"Shopping?" This was getting better.

"Then we'll spend some time with the kids when we get back. We'll take a few trips with them to show them the work we're doing in other countries. I'm looking forward to seeing the new well."

Princess Ava was thinking about her wardrobe. Her closet was bulging with old clothes, shoes, and accessories. How could she venture out in public wearing these old things? They were fine for wearing around the castle or her interview with Jill, but now they'd be hobnobbing with European royals. Shopping would be essential.

Working on the computer was boring. She was beginning to regret offering to help her husband with his charitable work. She really wanted to get back to her book and find out what happened between the pirate and the maiden. Maybe he'd let her take a break soon.

She hardly ever checked her email, but idly clicked on it so she could escape the mind-numbing data entry she was doing. As usual, there were a bunch of junk emails she began deleting. There were a few interspersed from the kids. She sent them quick responses. Then she noticed the one from Jill. Actually, there were several from Jill. She read the oldest one first.

Dear Princess Ava,

Thank you so much for indulging me with your time and hospitality. I didn't expect the interview to take so long, but I must admit, I enjoyed my stay in your town. I'm hoping to have the article completed within a week. Unfortunately, I'm unable to give you editorial approval. This is the magazine's policy.

Sincerely,
Jill

Princess Ava was feeling anxious about the article. She was confident she'd been able to pull off perpetuating their fairy tale story, but now she was plagued by feelings of dread and regret. Maybe her husband's reticence had rubbed off on her. Why had she agreed to do this silly interview and risk revealing the truth? It would be beyond humiliating if the public knew they were in therapy.

Jill was a serious journalist. She'd know how to dig around for the truth, but why had she pursued this story in the first place? It puzzled her. She opened the next email.

Dear Princess Ava,

I was able to do more interviews to round out the article, and it's almost completed. I hope you'll be satisfied with the final version. I'm attaching the photo I took of you and Prince Kellan in the royal gardens. It will be published along with the article. It's a beautiful photo, and I'm very pleased with it. I think you will be, too.

By the way, is there anywhere I can get some of those delicious pastries or are they only available at the castle?

Sincerely,
Jill

Princess Ava opened the picture. It was indeed beautiful with the background of the gardens. She and Prince Kellan stood turned slightly toward each other. Her head was tilted coyly towards him, and they were both smiling happily. The sun brought out golden highlights in her hair, and it fell perfectly around her face and over her shoulders. Her jewelry and tiara sparkled, and her dress was flattering. Very nice indeed.

But wait! Who else had Jill interviewed? She knew about Agnes, but who else had she tracked down? This was not good and unsettled her.

Dear Princess Ava,

I haven't heard from you. I hope you're getting my emails. My apologies if you're too busy to respond. The article is complete and is scheduled to be published in our next issue. I'll have it sent to you right off the presses. Again, thank you so much for your time and graciousness. Please tell Prince Kellan that I also appreciate his time and will include a link to the Royal Charitable Trust in the article. Hopefully, it will bring his work some recognition, publicity, and donations.

Also, can you tell me where I can purchase some of those pastries? Best wishes, and I sincerely hope you and Prince Kellan live happily ever after.

Sincerely,
Jill

The emails sounded friendly enough, but Princess Ava was still feeling uneasy about the article. She knew her husband would be pleased with the link to the trust, especially if it brought in a few donations. He was always going on about the need for continued funding for his endless projects. This could be the silver lining of the ominous cloud that was this article.

Get a grip, she told herself. It might not be that bad. Jill might write a flattering article. Probably not, but what was the worst that could happen? All her secrets would be revealed, and she'd die of embarrassment. There could be a royal scandal, and those European royals would look down on them. She'd feel horrible if she ruined the royal family's reputation. Then Prince Kellan would have to divorce her to save face. Oh, my gosh! It could all go terribly wrong, and the cascading effects could devastate her entire life. That's all!

She had to respond to Jill. She was shaking as she thought about what to type back. There had to be subtle ways to influence her to be kind and discreet. Princess Ava could emphasize the importance of the trust. Jill had seemed impressed with it and would see the necessity for a more positive spin.

Dear Jill,

Thank you for your emails. The picture was lovely. I'm looking forward to reading your article. I know you will be fair and understand the importance of a certain discretion. Prince Kellan will be quite pleased with the link to the Royal Charitable Trust. We have been working together diligently to bring about some positive changes to poverty-stricken areas of the world. This is the most important thing to both of us.

I enjoyed our conversations and felt like I was talking to a friend. I hope your readers enjoy the story of our true-life fairy tale. My wish is that it will give them hope for their own dreams and that they will all find their own princes someday. I hope you find yours. The pastries are baked right here in the castle, and I'd be happy to have some sent to you.

Sincerely,
Princess Ava

She hesitated before hitting Send. Mentioning the trust might make Jill rethink anything in the article that would be hurtful to her or her husband and jeopardize the Royal Charitable Trust. Prince Kellan would never forgive her if she damaged the reputation of the trust.

She had also hinted at using discretion and conversing as friends. Friends don't betray each other, but when were journalists ever discreet? Their friendly maneuverings were usually employed to get a story. She so didn't want this to go badly, but an uneasy feeling taunted her.

19 A Strange Twist

Ava couldn't quite remember where she was when she opened her eyes. It felt like she was sleeping on a soft cloud. A ray of sunlight had fallen across the bed and woken her. She turned over and fell back asleep until the sound of tapping roused her again.

"Are you awake, Ava?" a female voice called through the door.

"Yes." She sat up and scanned the room in the light of day. She wasn't home. She wasn't at the inn. She wasn't in the woods with Kent. They had gotten caught and were in trouble, and she had spent the night in this luxurious room in the castle. And now they had to accept the consequences.

Cora peeked her head into the room. "You're awake. Why don't you get dressed, and I'll come back and get you for breakfast?"

That sounded wonderful. Ava's stomach felt awfully empty.

"Is Kent okay?" she asked anxiously. Had they had him arrested?

"Who?" Cora asked.

"My friend. The one I was with last night."

Cora smiled. "He's just fine. Get dressed. I'll be back in a few minutes." She closed the door.

What a relief. It didn't seem like they were in trouble. The staff might just let them go and not tell anyone. Maybe the royal family didn't even know there were intruders under their roof. She'd feel better once she saw that Kent was okay. Then they could go get the car, and she could meet his parents.

Ava donned clean clothes from her backpack, even though they were wrinkled. Then she made the bed out of habit. She sat on it and waited for Cora to return. It was strange to think that the Prince was probably somewhere in the castle right now. And so was Kent.

Cora knocked on the door, and once again led her down long hallways and a flight of stairs. Ava followed, carrying her backpack. She tried to glance into rooms they passed but saw no one.

Cora led her into a small sunroom with a wooden table and chairs. There was a covered plate on a placemat. A glass of orange juice, a pot of tea, and a basket of warm rolls were also on the table. There was only one place set. She had hoped to see Kent. Why were they keeping them apart? She set her backpack down and looked at Cora with concern.

"Where's my friend? I need to see my friend," she insisted. "Are you sure he's okay?"

"He's fine," Cora assured her. "Now, why don't you sit down and eat? You must be hungry."

"But where is he? Isn't he going to eat too?"

Ava pulled out the chair and sat down. Something smelled delicious. She lifted the cover from the plate to reveal scrambled eggs and potatoes. She looked up, but Cora was already gone. She resolved to find Kent as soon as she finished eating.

It didn't take long for her to ingest the eggs, potatoes, two rolls and orange juice. She poured some tea and sat in the sunroom, waiting for someone to come and get her. She'd eaten alone, admiring the view of the royal gardens out the window. She thought how nice it would be to do this every day.

She wondered where the royal family was eating breakfast. The Prince was somewhere in this castle, perhaps also staring out at the gardens. This place was so big, she couldn't get her bearings. And where was Kent? Why wouldn't they let them see each other? It made her anxious. Was this some sort of tactic to see if their stories matched?

It had been a stupid idea to break into the gardens just to make a wish at the wishing well. Why had she gone along with it? It must've taken them way out of their way. Yet she'd spent the night in the castle, and here she was eating breakfast in the castle. She couldn't imagine this happening to very many people. It was probably as close as she'd ever get to her dream of living here.

Why hadn't she wished to meet the Prince and live happily ever after in the castle at the well? Instead, her wishes had been about Kent. She really did love him, even if he couldn't give her much. Love was so impractical.

She got up and sat on the padded window seat, gazing out at the flowers glistening with morning dew. At least she was rested, and her stomach was full before they had to set out again. If they let them go. They could still be in serious trouble.

She heard the door open and looked up. It was Kent! He looked different. His baseball hat was gone, and his hair was shiny and curly. He was clean shaven and wore clean clothing. She smiled with relief.

"I was so worried about you," she said. "Are you okay? They wouldn't let me see you."

"I know. I'm okay. Are you?" He came over and sat beside her, taking her hand.

"I'm fine. I slept in the most comfortable bed I've ever been in, and breakfast was delicious," she marveled. "I just wish you could've eaten with me. Did you eat yet?"

"Yes. I ate." He gently kissed her. "I missed you last night."

"I missed you too," she said fervently. "I wish they wouldn't have separated us."

"They're very proper here," he answered.

Ava sighed. "Isn't it beautiful?" she asked as she looked out at the flowers. "It must be nice to see this every day. It's so peaceful."

Kent followed her gaze. "If you had the chance,

you'd rather live here with the Prince, wouldn't you?"

She looked at him with surprise. "I told you I didn't send in my picture. I want to be with you."

"But, if you had the chance, you'd want to meet the Prince," he persisted.

"I met him at the ball."

"But there were hundreds of girls and everyone had masks on."

"What are you trying to say? Does the Prince want to meet us?"

"Do you want to meet him?" he asked back.

"I chose you," she insisted, but her heart beat faster.

"I think this is what you really want," he said solemnly.

"Kent," she said. "At the well, I wished for you, for us, for our future."

But she wavered a bit. Why was he pushing her away? Is this why he'd brought her to the castle? Because he thought she wanted to meet the Prince?

Ava looked down at her wrinkled clothes. She didn't feel presentable. What if this was it? What if this was her moment? Her destiny? What if everything had led her here? She looked up at Kent. Was he the sacrifice she had to make?

He seemed a bit disheartened. He must be afraid of losing her, but didn't want to stand in her way. Maybe he also sensed that this was her destiny. But she didn't want to lose him. She really didn't. Would fate twist them away from each other? Was it out of her hands?

Ava looked into Kent's eyes and saw sadness. What more could she say to convince him? It had been his idea to come to the royal gardens and find the wishing well to wish upon. It wasn't her fault they'd been caught and brought to the castle. Yet he was acting like she'd deceived him.

He turned away from her. "I know you want to

meet the Prince. That's why you went to the ball. That's why you know Agnes. She helped you."

"How do you know Agnes?" she demanded. "Tell me the truth. Was she your fairy godmother too? Do guys have fairy godmothers or would it be fairy godfathers?"

Somehow that didn't sound right.

He laughed despite himself. "No. At least I don't think so." He shook his head. "We're getting off the subject."

He stood with a decisive look on his face.

"Where are you going?" she asked anxiously. "Please don't leave me again."

"I promise I won't leave you," he vowed. "I believe you, Ava. I feel a connection with you, and I believe you when you say I'm the one that you want. I'm sorry I'm so mistrusting."

"I'm glad you believe me, Kent." She felt relieved. "Are they going to let us go now?"

"It's okay. We're not prisoners," he assured her. "I didn't tell you much about myself, but now I'd like you to meet my parents."

Ava was puzzled. "Do your parents work here?"

He smiled. "Yes. That's right. I'm just going to go talk to them for a few minutes, and then you can meet them." He gave her a quick kiss and left her alone again.

This explained why the staff was being so nice to them, and they weren't in trouble for trespassing. It also explained how Kent knew about the wishing well. She wondered if he'd grown up in the staff quarters here. He'd probably always felt overshadowed by the Prince. No wonder he was so touchy about it.

What a beautiful place to live, even if you were working. She wouldn't mind being a maid in a place like this. They must have a huge, well-paid staff. With her experience, she could probably get a job here if things didn't work out with Kent. But it wouldn't come to that. Their future would be filled with adventure and romance. That was what she'd signed up for.

She was a little nervous at the prospect of meeting Kent's parents. She'd never been introduced to a boy's parents before. She hoped they liked her. Maybe she and Kent could stay and work here just until they had enough money to travel. She'd suggest this to him. She sure wouldn't mind sleeping in that comfortable bed again, although she'd rather sleep beside him. It made her feel safer. She'd never imagined being in the castle in this way. Life was certainly full of strange twists.

Cora entered the room and smiled at her. Was this his mother? Ava jumped to her feet. Cora motioned for her to follow her. Ava timidly traipsed behind her. What if they didn't like her? What if they'd had higher hopes for their son? It was so nerve-racking.

Cora led her up some stairs and down a long hall. Then they went up more stairs and down another long hall. Ava was getting more apprehensive with each step. Where was Kent? Why hadn't he come and gotten her himself? It would've made her feel much calmer.

Cora suddenly stopped before a closed door. "Wait here."

She went in and closed the door behind her. After a few minutes, she reappeared standing before Ava beaming. She brushed the wrinkles out of Ava's shirt with her hands and combed through her hair with her fingers.

"There," she said, looking at Ava maternally. "Now, don't be nervous. Just remember to curtsy."

Curtsy? She didn't know how to curtsy. Why would she have to curtsy?

"Where's Kent?" she asked desperately.

Cora looked confused. "Who?"

"My friend. Where's my friend?" she asked insistently.

Did Cora think she was someone else? Was this some kind of mistake? Something was wrong.

"Oh, your friend. Yes. He's already inside." Cora smiled kindly at her again. "Go on. They're waiting." She turned the knob and opened the door for Ava.

Ava stepped into a sitting room. She was in a daze. Everything from the drapes to the carpet to the furniture to the people sitting on the couch was lavish and rich looking. It took her a moment to notice the crowns on their heads. This had to be a mistake. She felt horrified and took a step back.

"Curtsy," Cora whispered loudly from the doorway.

Then she heard the door close. She bowed clumsily.

"I'm so sorry," she mumbled. "This must be a mistake. I shouldn't be here. I'm so sorry."

"Sit down, my dear," the Queen ordered.

Ava was trembling all over. She plopped down on a flowered settee before her knees gave out. She was sure she'd violate the protocol and further embarrass herself. With her head down, she peeked at Queen Aurora and King Kellan. Then she noticed the third person sitting on the other side of the King in a cushioned chair. He wore a smaller crown on his dark curly hair. It couldn't be! Could it? The Prince and Kent could be twins.

He stood and approached her. "I'm sorry I had to lie to you. I had to be sure it was me you wanted and not all this." He gestured around the room.

Ava suddenly felt faint. This was surely a dream.

Kent extended his hand and pulled her to her feet. They stood side-by-side facing his parents. He squeezed her hand, and it gave her a bit of comfort.

"Mom. Dad. This is Ava. I danced with her at the

ball. I told you I'd explain everything when you met her. I ran away because I didn't want to be matched with someone who wouldn't love me for who I am, but only for what I could offer. Ava didn't know who I was. We spent a great deal of time together and talked about our hopes and dreams, and we fell in love. She thought I had nothing, but she stuck with me. I'm convinced that she loves *me*."

The Queen and King exchanged looks.

"How old are you?" Queen Aurora asked her.

"I'm almost eighteen," Ava answered in a shaky voice.

"Do you go to the high school?" King Kellan asked.

She shook her head. "No, sir. I mean, Your Highness."

"Who's your family?" the Queen asked.

"My stepmother owns the inn. That's where I was working when I met..." Her voice trailed off.

Now they knew she was nothing more than a maid and would find her unsuitable. Why had she opened her big mouth?

"I see," said the Queen. "And what were your plans before you met my son?"

To marry the Prince? She couldn't say that. Her mind went blank.

"I don't know," Ava answered shyly. "I guess I didn't have any plans yet."

The King glanced at the Queen and then looked at Ava. "Well, young lady, we're very grateful you have returned our son to us."

"Oh, I didn't..." Ava started to say, but Kent squeezed her hand.

It was so odd. Everything had changed. Nothing had been as it had seemed. She had to adjust the way she viewed Kent. Apparently, he was really the Prince. He was Prince Kellan. She couldn't even wrap her mind around this.

Had Agnes known? She thought back. She didn't think so until she'd come upon them in the woods. She had seemed to recognize him then. Now Ava felt intimidated by him and especially by his parents. Oh, my gosh! She was standing in the castle before the King and the Queen holding the Prince's hand!

20 The Truth Behind the Fairy Tale

Princess Ava fidgeted in Dr. Tucker's office. She was on time and had been helping Prince Kellan as promised, but she'd had a terrible dream the night before. Sleep had been eluding her since she'd read Jill's emails, and now her dreams were turning dark, churning up insecurities from the past.

She'd dreamed she was back working at the inn. She'd protested to Hazel that she was a princess now, and somebody else was supposed to do all the work. But then Agnes had appeared and told her she had undone the spell, and everything had reverted to the way it was before. The Prince had married someone else. Ava asked why. Why had this happened? Agnes and Hazel shook their heads at her.

"You never should've done that interview," they replied in unison.

"I'm sorry," Princess Ava said out loud.

Prince Kellan and Dr. Tucker looked at each other.

"About what?" her husband asked her.

"Oh." She snapped back to the present. "Nothing. I was just thinking."

"Something is clearly bothering you," Dr. Tucker observed. "You're in a safe environment. Why don't you tell us what it is?"

She looked from Dr. Tucker to Prince Kellan. A sense of guilt had also descended upon her.

Her husband took her hand. "What is it? Tell me," he urged. "We're in this together. It can't be that bad."

"Well." She debated whether to share her fears. "I'm a little worried about the article."

Prince Kellan laughed. "Is that all?"

"Why don't you tell us what you're worried

about?" Dr. Tucker suggested.

"I guess I'm afraid that the article might differ from what I told her. She may not have believed me." She bit her lip.

They both waited for her to elaborate. Then Prince Kellan shook his head.

"I told you not to do it. What kind of story did you feed her?"

"What you mean?" she asked defensively.

"What you're afraid of is that she's going to find out the truth because you made up some outlandish fairy tale." He shook his head. "You told her a story just like one of your books, didn't you?"

"I tried to stick to the fairy tale because it's true," she asserted. "More or less."

"Nobody believes that story," Prince Kellan said dismissively.

"I do," she answered.

"That's ridiculous. You were there. You know it's not true."

"Well, most of it is. Some of it is," she retorted. "I want it to be."

"What specifically do you want to be true that isn't?" Dr. Tucker interjected.

"What? I'm not romantic enough for you? Are you going to start that again?" Prince Kellan dropped her hand.

"What's wrong with romance?" she wailed.

"It's like a drug for her," her husband said to Dr. Tucker. "I can never live up to those books."

"Ava," Dr. Tucker said calmly. "Go ahead and explain to us what your fears are about the article."

"I just... I just want people to see us as the ideal couple in the fairy tale that was based on our lives," she stammered. "We're supposed to be the perfect couple. We're supposed to live happily ever after."

"And how do you feel about the reality?" Dr. Tucker persisted.

"I don't know." She looked down at her hands. She just couldn't seem to clarify it for them.

"Seriously? You're going to tell me you're not happy?" Her husband asked impatiently. "You have everything anyone could ever want. I can't believe you."

"Kellan, let's not judge. Your wife has to feel safe here in order to be honest," Dr. Tucker said patiently. "Ava, try to put into words what you're feeling."

"Maybe I *am* too worried about appearances," she admitted. "I just don't want everyone to know about our problems. I don't even know why we have problems. I want things to be the way they were in the beginning."

"You expect things to be too perfect just like in your books, but that's not reality," Prince Kellan said harshly. "You have some crazy fantasy about how life is supposed to be. Just accept things the way they are. We have a great life. We're very lucky."

"I know," she said. Why did she often feel like he was lecturing her? "I don't know why we keep talking about my books. I enjoy reading them. What's wrong with that? Besides, I was talking about the article. I feel nervous about it."

"Let's get back to that," Dr. Tucker agreed. "Share what you're feeling, Ava."

"Why did you do the interview in the first place if you're so nervous about the truth coming out?" Prince Kellan asked with irritation.

"I don't know." Princess Ava looked down at her hands in her lap again.

Had they just gone around in circles? And why did her books so threaten her husband? Could it be he felt jealous of the men in these stories? Did he feel he was competing with them? Years ago, she'd chosen him. He must know that he'd always been her first choice. Her only choice. Her happily ever after choice.

~~~

It was raining. Princess Ava reclined in the library that was filled with shelves of beloved books. She had one opened tantalizingly on her lap with her favorite mug filled with green tea beside her. On a white plate sat a cinnamon muffin. But she couldn't concentrate and watched raindrops running down the windowpane. The rain was good for the gardens.

A rainbow would soon stretch across the sky, compliments of Agnes. At their wedding, Agnes had promised her a rainbow every day in the afternoon. Her magical powers had always been erratic, but she'd delivered on the promise of this special wedding gift.

The door suddenly creaked open, and in toddled her in-laws.

Queen Aurora addressed her. "Is this where we're receiving the Ambassador?"

"Uh." Sometimes Princess Ava wasn't sure how to deal with them. "Yes. Come in and have a seat."

It was probably best to humor them. She wondered why they were wandering around unattended. Someone was always supposed to be with them, but they seemed to slip away at times.

They settled themselves onto a couch.

"Where is Cora?" the Queen asked. "I must have my coffee. Do you want something?" She turned to King Kellan.

"Let's not spoil our dinner." He smiled the same smile that Prince Kellan had.

Cora had retired years ago, but it would only confuse them if Princess Ava tried to remind them. She realized they were both looking at her expectantly.

"It's raining," was all she could think to say.
~~~

"Lovely for the flowers." Queen Aurora smiled.

"Yes. Yes. Lovely," the King nodded and repeated.

"The children will be home to visit soon," Princess Ava offered. "Do you remember your grandchildren?"

"Grandchildren!" King Kellan exclaimed. "First the boy must marry."

"He's much too young," the Queen said.

"Give him a few years," the King added. They nodded in agreement.

Princess Ava sighed. It was nice for them that they lived in the past together.

Prince Kellan poked his head in the room. "There they are."

"Kellan, I've been looking all over for you!" his mother exclaimed. "Now don't wander off again. Cora has her hands full."

Prince Kellan shook his head and smiled at Princess Ava. "Okay, Mom. I won't." He sat next to his wife. "What are we talking about?"

"You're too young to get married," she said.

"Ah. I knew I was too young for you." He grinned.

She had to smile despite a feeling of melancholy. Perhaps it was the rain.

Susan pushed open the door that had been left ajar. "Oh, you're all in here," she said with surprise. "You received a package, Princess." She handed a large envelope to her.

"Thank you, Susan."

Princess Ava looked at the return address. It was from *Modern Woman's World* magazine. It must be the issue with the article!

"Would you like me to take them?" Susan gestured toward the King and Queen.

"They're fine right here," Prince Kellan said.

"Can you bring the Queen her coffee?" Princess Ava asked.

"Of course. Right away." Susan hurried out.

Princess Ava ripped open the envelope and pulled out the magazine. The cover showed a woman in a business suit holding a briefcase and a small child. She read the blurbs on the cover.

"Top 20 Women Entrepreneurs." "Family Friendly Vacations." "How to Get Paid What You're Worth." "Happily Ever After? The Truth Behind the Fairy Tale."

Princess Ava's eyes widened. What had Jill uncovered? A feeling of alarm filled her as she stared at the cover.

"Well, aren't you going to read it?" Prince Kellan asked.

She turned to the table of contents. The story was on page twenty-three. She found that page. There was the picture of the two of them in the garden that Jill had emailed to her with a smaller photo of the children inset at the bottom.

"That's a great picture of us." Prince Kellan tilted his head to see it.

Princess Ava was busy reading the article, and he read along with her.

Happily Ever After? The Truth Behind the Fairy Tale
By Jill Graham

If you're like me, you grew up with fairy tales. From movies to books, we were fed the fantasy of happily ever after. Girls, especially, were led to believe that all we had to do was be pretty and good, and a charming prince would rescue us from the ordinary and sweep us off our feet. But there aren't enough princes to go around, and we eventually figure out that we must "settle" for a real man who falls drastically short of this ideal. Is this harmless fantasy or are we the victims of brainwashing?

Modern women struggle with the expectation to have it

all. We want a career and a family with the love of our life. We're conditioned to believe it's achievable and essential to our happiness, but we're finding out that this is not an easy or reasonable balancing act. Divorce has become commonplace, which indicates the disappointment that plagues us. So how do we reconcile the dream with reality?

And then I got to wondering. Whatever happened to the real princess in the story? Did she live happily ever after as we're led to believe? The story ends as the Prince and the Princess marry and embark on a bliss-filled future. Or so we assume.

It was time for me to go to the source and find the Princess whose real-life story started it all. I set out for the tiny storybook town of Quimby, which is nestled in a hidden valley in the commonwealth territory of Wellstonia. Our Princess Ava was an ordinary young woman rescued from a life of drudgery by her handsome Prince Kellan. The story goes that her mother died, and her father remarried a woman who treated her like an unpaid servant. Young Ava, with the help of her fairy godmother, attended the royal ball where the Prince fell instantly in love with her. She fled the ball, fearing that the spell would wear off before he could find out her name. Yet our prince did not give up so easily. He searched high and low for the love he'd found. And the story resolves in a romantic climax that makes women sigh and men roll their eyes. Have we all been wronged? Have our vastly different expectations marred our chances for a truer happiness together?

I arrived in the picturesque town of Quimby to find it's as small and quaint as you'd imagine. Princess Ava is lovely and beautiful and gracious. Every day she wore a different gown and blinded me with glittering jewelry. Upon her silken blonde hair sat a perpetually sparkling tiara. She was happy to promote the fairy tale as truth and appears to live in an oblivious, romantic bubble. Not that I can blame her. Her prince is more than charming. He is amazingly handsome in an effortless way. He pours most of his time and energy into the Royal Charitable Trust, which is sponsoring many humanitarian projects all over the globe. I found his devotion to these critical endeavors impressive and sincere. (Learn more and donate by clicking the link at the end of this article.)

However, I sensed not all was as perfect as it seemed. It appeared too good to be true. But was that just the cynic in me? I put my journalistic skills to use to search for the truth behind the fairy tale. I dug in the local library and sought all the major players to piece together a more accurate version of this happily ever after tale.

I began with Princess Ava's "stepmother." Hazel was more than happy to speak with me as she feels she's gotten a bad rap. Fallacy #1 was revealed when she explained that Ava's mother did not die. Instead, she ran off with Hazel's husband when Ava was a teenager. Therefore, Hazel and Ava's father never married. She told me how troubled Ava was. Hazel often found her talking to birds and other animals, insisting that she could communicate with them. For her own protection, Hazel kept her out of school and employed her at her inn where she could monitor her. She feels that Princess Ava turned her back on her once she found her prince and has remained ungrateful ever after.

Princess Ava's father, Howard, was welcomed at the castle where he lived until his passing. Her mother, Iris, turned up at the wedding and, apparently, had a last falling out with the Princess. She then disappeared again, not to be seen since. Hazel sold the inn years ago and retired. It's now known as the Quimby Bed & Breakfast, which is where I stayed. An impressive portrait of Hazel and her two beloved dogs, Elvis and Priscilla, hangs in the small lobby. I found the inn to be cozy and reasonably priced, with many local shops within walking distance.

Through a stroke of luck, I tracked down Ava's fairy godmother, Agnes, right before my departure. She's not what you'd imagine. She's rather coarse and frumpy and has also been retired for some time. She described Ava as a pretty, young girl who desperately wanted a better life. Her lack of education or any discernible skills left her with few options. However, she had a great desire and firm belief that it was her destiny to live in the castle. Agnes described Ava's steadfast determination and single-minded ambition to reach her goal. Agnes used her magical skills to create the ball gown and coach that transported Ava to that fateful royal ball, though she insists magic cannot make two people fall in love. Love holds a magic all its own. Agnes seemed quite protective and maternal towards Princess Ava, despite not seeing each other often. She alluded to their sometimes-rocky relationship while insisting that they remain close. Agnes also admitted to a fling with Princess Ava's father, Howard, and helped care for him while he was ill.

I saw this time with Agnes as presenting a unique opportunity to learn more about the sisterhood of fairy godmothers. Agnes sadly related that it has become a dying art. I wondered if every girl has her own fairy godmother waiting in the wings to help her achieve her dreams. Agnes told me that the process is highly selective, and she couldn't divulge this information.

However, it appears there are fewer and fewer out in the field, and, perhaps, that explains our frustrations. I gathered that fairy godmothers serve as mentors to young girls with a splash of magic thrown in to expedite matters. I also asked Agnes about Princess Ava's communications with animals and birds. Had Hazel's accusation been accurate, or did this place hold particular magic? Agnes seemed perplexed by this question. She takes the existence of magic in stride and corroborated that young Ava could communicate with other living creatures. I wondered how Princess Ava had been chosen to be mentored, and Agnes vaguely explained that they had fatefully crossed paths three times. One must pay attention to these signs, she insisted.

Princess Ava painted a more idyllic and romantic story of true everlasting love with her prince. Their meeting was fateful, their attraction instant, their romance true. Their wedding was the cherry on the cake of her dreams. They have three children who attend a private school in Switzerland and visit home infrequently. Unfortunately, Queen Aurora and King Kellan have descended into dementia. Many of us are in the same position with our parents. We can certainly empathize, though Princess Ava vehemently disavows any detail that would mar the illusion of perfection she has carefully cultivated. Yet her storybook life is not so different from any other dysfunctional family. She doesn't realize we'd love her all the more if she allowed us a glimpse of her flaws and the drawbacks of life in the castle. It'd certainly make us feel more comfortable with our own messy lives.

I also interviewed some of the staff in the castle on condition of anonymity. Their comments about the Princess were not flattering. She was described as superficial and obsessed with her appearance. She is sometimes short with the staff while the Prince is always polite. She is an avid reader of romance novels and is obsessed with perpetuating the fairy tale fantasy. Ironically, she and the Prince seem to live separate lives. Prince Kellan spends most of his time in his office diligently saving the world while Princess Ava wanders aimlessly in the castle or the royal gardens, struggling with boredom. Possibly, they have grown apart as many couples do. This we can forgive them as many of us can relate.

We may never know the full truth of this couple's story, and, perhaps, we shouldn't. Their private lives should remain private to a certain extent, despite their celebrity. Their story has long been romanticized and idealized in fiction. It's easy to become disenchanted with this tale of exaggerations and fabrications, but I believe their love is genuine, and I believe their problems are human. They may not be perfect, and we shouldn't expect them to be. Princess Ava is flawed, but I liked her and sympathized with her efforts to perpetuate the dream. Any way you look at it, she ended up with her prince, and I hope they find their way back to their happily ever after. Each of our princes will be imperfect as we are ourselves, but we must still believe in love and romance and a bit of magic. I still choose to believe. I hope you do too. ~JG

"That wasn't so bad," Prince Kellan stated. "This will give the trust some publicity."

Princess Ava sat with the magazine open on her lap, staring down at it. A drip splattered onto the page. And that's when he saw her tears.

"I sound awful." Her voice faltered. "I sound shallow and self-centered and horrible and stupid."

"It's just a magazine article," he said flippantly. "It's not a big deal. It will blow over."

"How could she write these things about me?" she moaned. "I thought she liked me."

"Journalists are always looking for dirt. Didn't it occur to you that she might say some negative things?"

Princess Ava shook her head. "I thought she'd just print what I told her."

"It's not that bad," he maintained.

"Not for you. She was sure captivated by you."

"That's because I'm the handsome prince in the story," he joked.

"This is humiliating." Princess Ava closed the magazine and tossed it onto the floor by the window.

"I never give interviews," the Queen intoned.

~~~

"I feel completely betrayed," Princess Ava admitted Dr. Tucker. "I trusted her. I told her what she wanted to hear. I told her the story. Everyone wants to believe the story."

Prince Kellan shook his head. "I don't know why you're so surprised. Jill was a journalist. I tried to warn you."

"I'm embarrassed," she said tearfully. "What will people think?"

"This is why we never do interviews," her husband reiterated.

"Why did you let me do this interview?" she demanded angrily.

"It's not my fault." He held up his hands.

"It may not feel like it now, but this will pass," Dr. Tucker assured her.

"They did a story on the local news." She dabbed at her eyes with a tissue. "It made me look like a selfish idiot. Now the magazine is everywhere."

"There's an upside. The trust has gotten a lot of donations," Prince Kellan said.
~~~

Princess Ava continued to pout.

"Let's try to put this into perspective," Dr. Tucker suggested. "There are much worse things that could happen. Nobody's sick and nobody died."

"I'm dying of embarrassment," she whined. "How can we take our trip now and face all those European royals?"

"They won't read that magazine in Europe," Prince Kellan reasoned. "Besides, do you think they all have clean slates? They're the worst. They have scandals all the time."

"Really?" She blew her nose.

"You're a real royal now." Prince Kellan chuckled.

"It still makes me mad. I'm going to send her an email."

"Best not to stir things up further," Dr. Tucker advised. "Let things settle down first. Time will pass, and the next issue will come out, and everyone will talk about something else."

"We have to plan our anniversary party," Prince Kellan said to distract her.

"Oh, my gosh. I have to finish the guest list and find a dress and decide on the menu. There's so much to do," Princess Ava remembered.

"We'll do it together," her husband offered.

"And I don't want the press there," she stated emphatically.

21 Magically a Princess

Ava was still in shock. She was trying to wrap her head around these recent revelations. She was alone with Prince Kellan in a small library. Books lined the walls from floor to ceiling. She thought how wonderful it would be to have your very own library. She could see the lush, rain-drenched gardens through the tall windows. She had to be dreaming.

"I'm sorry I lied to you," he said. "I just had to be sure."

"I understand," she answered numbly.

"I want you to call your father and Hazel to let them know you're okay."

Ava scowled.

"Well, at least call your father. He's probably worried, and I don't want them filing a missing persons report," he reasoned.

"Okay," she agreed. "What happens now? I mean, are we still going to travel and do the things we talked about?"

"Unfortunately, I can't change who I am. I wish I could live a normal life, but I was born into this and, as the first-born son, I have certain responsibilities." He gave her a weak smile.

"First born?"

"Yes. My brother was lucky. The only thing he has to worry about is not creating a scandal. He gets to play all over the world and lives in Switzerland most of the time. That's where we went to a special school for royal children," he explained. "So, if you choose to stay with me, we're kind of stuck here most of the time."

"Of course I want to stay with you, Kent!" she cried. "Wait. What should I call you?"

Ava was unfamiliar with the protocol. It was all so surreal. She'd dreamed of this her entire life, and now here she was. The reality was jolting.

"My name is Kellan. I liked Superman when I was little, so I used the name Kent Clark."

"Huh?" She didn't get it. Her thoughts were too scattered.

"We'll send for your things, and you can stay in the same room you stayed in last night until..."

"Until?" she repeated.

What now? Had the King and Queen rejected her? Was he going to send her back to the inn?

He grinned at her.

"What?" she asked.

And then Prince Kellan dropped onto one knee and took her hand. He smiled up at her, and she noticed the cute freckles on the bridge of his nose again.

"Ava, will you do me the honor of becoming my wife and my princess and live and love with me happily ever after in this castle?"

Ava began trembling, and tears blurred her vision. She was surely dreaming. That elusive castle shimmering against the horizon had taunted her at every turn. Yet she'd believed so long in her destiny, even when fate had twisted it from her grasp so many times, that it didn't seem real that she was standing inside that castle and the Prince was kneeling before her. For a moment, she couldn't speak and time stood still.

Finally, she mumbled, "Okay."

~~~

It was Ava's wedding day. By the end of the day, it would be official and she would be a princess. The Queen had taken to organizing the entire event despite her initial resistance to the marriage, but Ava didn't mind. She picked out the beautiful cream lace gown and the dainty headdress with the veil. Her hair flowed over her shoulders and down her back in
~~~

soft curls. Perfection achieved.

Butterflies jumped erratically in her stomach. There were so many guests, most of whom she didn't know. Ava would meet Kellan's brother for the first time. Agnes was invited, of course. Kellan had convinced her to invite her parents and their significant others. It had taken some doing to track down her mother. She'd been in Arizona all this time.

Agnes and Ava's mother, Iris, fussed over her. They seemed competitive over her. Ava wondered if her parents would even speak to each other. It was such a soap opera. She didn't want anything to go wrong. The day had to be absolutely perfect, just as she had dreamed it a million times.

Kellan's brother, Kerrson, was the best man. He was named after Queen Aurora's father. She'd struggled with her choice for maid of honor. It was between her mother and Agnes. Her mother had abandoned her, and Agnes had been there for her. But her mother was her mother. Family. Loyalty. Friendship. Which of these trumped the others? She asked Kellan for his opinion, but he was no help. He said it was up to her. So, she thought long and hard about it. She vacillated back and forth. It had to be her mother. No, Agnes had been there for her. But her mother would be terribly hurt if she didn't choose her. But Agnes deserved the honor more. What to do?

She finally decided on her mother if they could find her. And they had. Agnes was upset.

"After all I've done for you?" she ranted. "You're like the daughter I never wanted. I mean, had. You know what I mean."

"I know. I know. But please try to get along with my mother. Don't turn her into anything." Ava hugged Agnes, who stiffened. She so missed her.

A flowered archway had been built in the royal gardens before a large fountain. Her father walked her down the pathway toward Kellan, who grinned happily at her. They'd kept the actual ceremony guest list small and intimate. The reception would be huge and overflowing with Kellan's relatives and friends of his parents. She stood before the fountain with Kellan and looked up to see Orville perched on a tree branch. What a happy day.

"From the moment I first saw you, I fell in love," Kellan read his vows to her. "I knew you were the one I wanted to go through life with and wanted to grow old with. Together, we will live and love and make the world a better place. We can weather any storms together, and forever we will be each other's shelter. I promise to always be truthful, and I promise you my undying love, Ava."

She looked down at the slip of paper in her hand. "Kellan," she looked into his eyes. "From the time I was a little girl, I always felt it was my destiny for us to be together. I felt drawn to you from the moment we met. I didn't know who you were, so I'm glad I listened to my heart and let it lead me because this is where I belong. This is a dream come true, and I love you and we will live happily ever after."

The minister read the traditional vows that they repeated to please the Queen. Then Kellan slipped the family ring onto Ava's finger, and they chastely kissed. And she was magically a princess.

The reception commenced in the main ballroom with a full orchestra. It was the same ballroom where they'd first danced. A roving photographer snapped his camera. They had agreed to release some approved photos to the media. The public loved royal weddings. Ava didn't know most of the guests. Kellan kept introducing her, but she instantly forgot their names and titles. It was a whirlwind of faces.

Kellan's brother, Kerrson, grabbed her into a big hug. He looked so much like Kellan. He had the same dark curly hair and dark eyebrows. He had the same smile, but he had a bit of a mischievous glint in his eyes.

"This is my brother, Prince Kerrson. We call him Kerr," Kellan said. "I see you've met."

"Welcome to the family." Kerr lifted his champagne glass to her and gulped down half of it. "We'll talk later, and I'll tell you all the family secrets." He laughed and went off to talk to someone.

She liked him instantly.

Ava hadn't had much time to talk to her mother, but she needed to. Questions nagged at her. She headed over to the family table. Unfortunately, her father and Hazel had been seated at the same table as her mother and Hazel's husband, Roger. Hazel was glaring at Iris.

Before she could reach the table, her mother rose and walked away. Hazel jumped up and went after her. They exchanged a barrage of angry words before Ava reached them.

"You shouldn't even be here," Hazel yelled at her mother. "How can you show your face?"

"I belong here more than you. I'm her mother. Not you," Iris hissed.

"Everyone knows you're a lying, backstabbing, selfish..."

"I'm not surprised Roger left you," Iris responded. "If you smiled, it'd crack your face."

Her father stood up. "Ladies, this is Ava's wedding. This is not the time..."

"Shut up, Howard." Iris turned on him. "When did you get a spine?"

Ava saw the hurt look on her father's face. How could her mother be so cruel?

"I was the one who took care of your daughter when you took off," Hazel said to Iris. "Howard never left her like you did."

"Mom." Ava hurried up to them. "Please, not here. Come with me."

Some of the other guests were staring at them. How mortifying. She led her mother outside where they could speak privately. She didn't know what to say. Years of feelings and questions were bottled up inside her.

"I'm sorry, sweetie. That nasty woman started it," her mother said.

"Mom." Ava tried to find the words. "What happened to you? I always thought you'd send for me, but all this time went by, and I never heard from you. Why did you leave me here like that?"

"Oh, sweetie. Look how it all turned out. I knew you'd be fine. I knew you were destined for better things." Her mother smiled at her.

"But why didn't I hear from you? You could've kept in touch to make sure I was okay."

"You know how it is. You get busy, and things happen, and time goes by." Iris shrugged.

"Do you know what my life was like after you left?" Ava demanded with rising anger. "I had to work at Hazel's inn. I was treated like a servant. It was awful. And poor Dad. He's really a good man."

"Your father? If he's so great, why did he get mixed up with Hazel and let her treat you that way?" Iris pointed a finger at her. "Your father is nothing but a doormat. I deserved better." She paced for a moment. "I'm sorry you were stuck with Hazel. I know how she is. Roger told me all about her."

"But what about me, Mom?" Ava whined. "You left me. We were close, and you just left me here. How could you do that to me?"

"I don't know what you want me to say here," Iris said with a frown.

"How about 'I'm sorry'? How about 'I should've never left you like that'?"

"Is that what this is all about? You just want me to say these things to you? What does it matter? I'm here now." She smirked. "I did what I had to do. I'm not going to apologize for it. Just get over it. It all turned out, so what difference does it make? I'm here for your big day."

Ava shook her head sadly. Now, finally, she'd seen her mother's true colors, and it wasn't pretty. She knew she wanted no more outbursts to ruin this wonderful day.

"I'm glad you were here today, Mom," Ava told Iris calmly. "I really am, but now I think that you and Roger need to leave."

Iris stared at her in disbelief. "Fine. Now you're a princess, and you're better than me. I get it." She turned and stormed off. She didn't get it at all.

Ava walked in the gardens a bit to compose herself. She was shaking. She'd seen another side of her mother, and it had slammed her into reality. She'd idolized Iris as a child. How different things seemed today.

"Hey, are you okay, kid?" It was Agnes.

"It was tough seeing my mother," she confessed.

"Families are the worst," Agnes acknowledged. "Did I tell you my sister is a witch? Don't get me started. I could tell you stories. Who doesn't have a crazy family?"

"I guess." Ava sighed.

"I like your father, but he has crappy taste in women. We were talking. He's a good listener, and he's funny. I accidentally slipped him my number." She covered her mouth with her hand. "Whoops."

"Did you really?" Ava raised her eyebrows.

"You bet I did. Howard just needs a little fun in his life, and who's more fun than me? I think he's kind of cute." She shrugged.

Ava hoped Agnes was right and her father could be happy. He surely deserved it. Maybe she'd invite him to live in the castle. Minus Hazel, of course.

"Anyway, I was going to say this during my toast, but I think you need it now," Agnes said. "I have a special gift for you. I had to work on this a long time, but I think I got it down."

"What is it?" Ava asked.

"These gardens are filled with magic. You feel it, right? Sometimes, if you look closely, you can see it in the air. It kind of twinkles," Agnes said. "This place magnifies my magical powers. It's pretty cool."

"I do feel it," Ava murmured. "I think I've always felt it."

"Magic only happens for those who believe," Agnes said. "Now look up, and you'll see my gift to you."

A vivid rainbow had materialized. It gleamed and glimmered above them.

"Agnes, it's the most beautiful thing I've ever seen," Ava whispered.

"This rainbow will appear every day at the same time as long as you believe," Agnes said. "Man, I'm good."

22 Perfect Fantasy

"I could turn her into... Wait. Let me think of something good." Agnes paced in front of the window.

"No. I don't want you to turn Jill into anything. She was just doing her job," Princess Ava said with resignation. She appreciated Agnes's loyalty. "Can you change the article or make it disappear from the magazine?"

"Can't do it. It's already out there," she answered. "I'd have to mess with time, and that's pretty tricky. I've never tried to do it. I don't think I'm powerful enough."

"I can't believe I trusted her," Princess Ava complained.

"You've always been gullible." Agnes pointed out. "Maybe my new boyfriend could do something. He's a wizard. I'll ask him tonight."

"New boyfriend? When did this happen?"

"I met him at a meeting last week. He's a hoot. I'll bring him around. He'll have you doubled over. I swear, he's hilarious." Agnes chuckled. "What were we talking about?"

"Jill wasn't nice to you either. She said you were coarse and frumpy," Princess Ava reminded her.

"I am coarse and frumpy," Agnes admitted. "Although I prefer to think of it as being direct and comfortable with myself. Semantics. Who cares?"

"At least you were loyal to me." Princess Ava sighed.

"I tried to talk you up to her, but, apparently, the staff isn't thrilled with you."

"Do you think I should I fire them?" Princess Ava mused.

"Nah. You don't know who said what," Agnes answered.

"I guess that's a little harsh. They work pretty

hard. I remember what it's like. I suppose I should be nicer to them."

"Never hurts."

"At least Jill didn't interview the kids. That's a relief."

"When are those little brats coming home? I miss them. Auntie Agnes wants some quality time with the little scamps."

"I know. I do, too," Princess Ava realized. "They're not so little anymore, and they've been running amok all over Europe. I don't know how Kellan keeps it out of the press."

"That guy's a keeper."

"Yes, he is." Princess Ava smiled.

"And what is this mysterious little smile?" Agnes noticed. "Is it happiness? As in happily ever after happiness?"

"Maybe," Princess Ava answered coyly.

~~~

"I know it wasn't good for you," Prince Kellan said to Princess Ava. "But the article has been great for the trust."

"That's fantastic."

Donations had quadrupled. For that, she was thankful.

She'd been working on the details of their anniversary bash. She'd never organized an event this large. The kids and their Uncle Kerr would fly in next week, and she was looking forward to it. Lately, she'd missed the kids more and more. And Kerr always livened things up when he was around.

Princess Ava studied her husband sitting at his computer working endlessly on behalf of the Royal Charitable Trust. She was glad something positive had come from the article. He was really a good person. He worked so tirelessly for people who
~~~

needed help. He'd always been like this. He'd always wanted to change the world for the better.

"Kell," she said.

"Hmm?" He was focusing on something on his computer.

"I've been thinking about our European vacation," she said slowly. "I don't think we should go now. We should spend time with the kids while they're home."

Prince Kellan looked up at her. "You're right. We can delay going to Europe for a few weeks. I'd like to see the kids more too. I miss them. I was thinking about keeping them home for a while. We could hire tutors for the girls, or maybe they should go to public school. It'd be good for them. K.C. can take online college courses."

"I like that idea," she said. "I have an idea, too."

"What is it?" He sounded distracted.

"I'd really like to see that well the trust paid for."

"Me too. We'll see it when we come back from Europe. We can take the kids. I'd like them to see it too," he said, tapping on his keyboard.

"I mean instead of going to Europe this summer." Princess Ava waited for the words to sink in.

The tapping stopped, and he swiveled his chair to face her. "Did you say instead of Europe?"

"I think we should all go see the well, and maybe some of the other projects. We should all be more involved." There. She'd said it.

"Are you sure that's what you want?" Disbelief laced his words.

"Absolutely." She nodded.

Prince Kellan's smile was exuberant, and his eyes filled with love. "That's the best thing I've heard you say since 'I do.'"

~~~
~~~

The sun was setting, and the sky was a spectacular amber. Prince Kellan sat beside Princess Ava on the bench and watched as the color deepened, and the sun went down, and the solar lanterns gradually lit up.

"Come with me. I want to show you something," he said.

"What is it?" she asked as he pulled her up and led her inside.

"I just want to ask your opinion on something. You're much better at decorating than I am. I made some changes to my room, and I wanted to know what you think."

"You want to ask me about decorating?" she asked with astonishment.

"Just tell me what you think," he said.

Princess Ava tried to come up with an acceptable response, just in case she didn't like his efforts. He didn't have a flair for decorating like she did, and she braced herself. The room would probably be done in dark depressing colors, unlike her bright cheery room.

He pushed open the door, and they stepped into his room. It was dark except for the glow of dozens of candles sending flickering light dancing along the walls. Throw pillows were scattered on his neatly made bed, and there was the subtle scent of vanilla wafting in the air.

Prince Kellan silently waited for her reaction. She put her hand to her mouth as she realized he was actually romancing her. It was overwhelming, and she turned to him and smiled warmly.

"Kellan," she murmured.

"Oh, fair maiden. You set me on fire with your dazzling beauty," he crooned. "Let me rip off my shirt so you can admire my rippling muscles."

Princess Ava giggled.

"And then I shall remove your dress and admire

your porcelain skin before I make mad passionate love to you." He grinned.

"Oh, Kell," she whispered as he drew her to him.

He stared longingly into her eyes for a moment, and she saw the love that ignited her deep desire for him. His kiss made her dizzy, and she shivered with yearning. Then he swept her up into his arms and carried her to his bed.

~~~

Princess Ava and Prince Kellan sat holding hands in Dr. Tucker's office. She was wearing a looser, more comfortable dress. They'd sold almost all the rest of her jewelry to benefit the trust. She felt happy and was looking forward to their trip with the kids. They'd even convinced Kerr to go with them.

"You two should be very proud of yourselves." Dr. Tucker beamed. "You've done the hard work and strengthened your relationship. I'm proud of you."

It hadn't been easy. Princess Ava had had to look at herself closely. A tough childhood had affected her confidence and feelings of security. It had been difficult to learn to think about others instead of her own survival. And she finally understood that everyone was flawed, and nothing was perfect.

She still liked to read her books, but she recognized they were fantasy, just like the fairy tale story about her and her prince. But the reality was not so bad. In fact, it was pretty wonderful.

"We've learned to communicate better," Prince Kellan was saying. "I think we always had a strong foundation of love, and that's what got us through. I admit I was a little jealous that my wife was fantasizing about these perfect men in her books, but I've gotten past it."

"I've really come to appreciate Kellan's devotion to his charitable projects through the trust. I think I
~~~

felt a little jealous of all the time he spent on it, but now I see how important it is. I want to work with him and make it a family effort," Princess Ava said. "My insecurities about the article were pretty trivial compared to the huge response we've gotten with donations. It was a small price to pay."

"Great news." Dr. Tucker nodded and closed his notepad.

"We've also opened the royal gardens back up to the public," she continued. "We'll have to keep some of it off limits, but it really belongs to the town, and everyone should be able to enjoy it."

"It'll be nice to see children playing in the gardens again," Prince Kellan added.

"Excellent. Our work together seems to be finished. I have full confidence that you can now handle anything that comes up together." Dr. Tucker stood. "I'm always here if you need me."

Prince Kellan shook his hand. "Thank you."

"Thank you, Dr. Tucker," Princess Ava said sincerely.

"Let's get some lunch," Prince Kellan said to her as they exited the office.

"I'll be right there," she . "I have to send a quick email."

Dear Jill,

I have to admit that I wasn't initially pleased with the way I was portrayed in the article, but the flood of donations for the Royal Charitable Trust has more than made up for it. I can't tell you how many people around the world have benefited. I am forever grateful.

The reason for this email is that I wanted to let you know that Prince Kellan and I will be taking a trip with our children to check on some of the projects that have been made possible because of these many generous donations. I'd like to invite you to join us to publicize the great work that we're doing. I hope you will consider writing an article about the Royal Charitable Trust and help us keep the donations coming.

Sincerely,
Princess Ava

P.S. I'll have more pastries sent to you.
P.P.S. The Prince has a brother.

~~~
~~~

Exclusive short story!

Sign up for the Book Bird newsletter and receive *The Interviews*

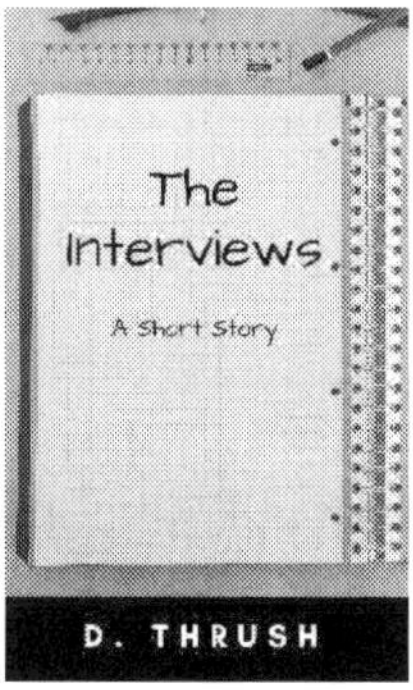

What's it like to be a fictional character? D. Thrush "interviews" the female protagonists of her books and then lets the male characters have their say. She said/he said! It was a little weird for D to hear some of their unexpected responses, not to mention the two who crashed the interviews uninvited! You don't have to be familiar with them to enjoy their thoughtful responses and lively banter.

https://landing.mailerlite.com/webforms/landing/m8v0s5

Why sign up? You'll find value in every newsletter whether it's freebies, sales, contests, inside news, info on new releases, or the opportunity to read ARCs (Advanced Reader Copies) and give your input on titles and covers. You'll only hear from me about once or twice a month and will be able to contact me directly. Join us and don't miss out on the fun!

From the Author

I hope you enjoyed ***Fairy Tale Karma***! This fun story teased my imagination for a long time, and I'm glad I can finally share it. I mixed a little realism, a touch of idealism, a bit of romance, and a sprinkling of magic into this story about how our childhoods affect us and how we can change. I like to use humor and balance it with heart and substance, and I hope I was able to achieve that.

I'm toying with the idea of writing a sequel featuring Agnes. Join my mailing list on the previous page or follow me on Amazon, BookBub or Goodreads for news about sales and new releases!

If you enjoyed this book, please post a rating or brief review on Amazon and/or Goodreads. I appreciate every one and it helps readers decide whether to read this book. Thank you! Here's the link for Amazon: **http://www.amazon.com/review/create-review?&asin=+BOOMOTHMPU**

What to read next? The description and first chapter of ***The Daughter Claus*** are on the following pages.

Each of my novels explores family and friendship, love and romance, relationships and life, and finding your power!

~*~*~*~*~*~*~*~*~*~*~*~*~

The Daughter Claus (Book 1)

Genres: Holiday Humor, Chick Lit

*****Wishing Shelf Award Finalist*****
*****Readers' Favorite Finalist*****

It's not all tinsel and candy canes for Santa's daughter!

Grumpy, workaholic Santa always favored Tina's younger brother, grooming him from birth to fill his boots when he retires. There's just one problem–Nicholas, Jr. hates Christmas. He even writes anti-Christmas songs for his rock band, *Black Ice*. When their father winds up in the hospital, it falls to Tina to leave college in sunny Florida and temporarily return home to the frozen North Pole to run the family business. Not only does she have to put her classes on hold, she has to leave a new romance with her brother's bandmate.

It isn't easy dealing with rowdy reindeer who enjoy karaoke, the ex-boyfriend who broke her heart, her best friend's flirtation with an elf, a long-distance relationship, and resistance from her father! Yet there's a bigger problem–Tina likes it. She excels at running the family business. But who will deliver the presents on Christmas Eve? Santa is supposed to be a man, right? Should Tina go back to college and her new love or fight to be the next Santa?

Christmas magic, girl power, and a dash of romance make this a fun story any time of year!

"My new favorite Christmas book. This is not the type of book I normally read. That being said, I LOVE this book." Amazon Customer

"Being Santa is not for sissies. I enjoyed this story. Will read it again." Marlowe K. Earl

"I even walked to the mailbox with my iPad in hand because I couldn't put it down." Amy

https://www.amazon.com/dp/B00M0THMPU

https://www.amazon.co.uk/dp/B00M0THMPU

Enjoy the first chapter next!

1 *Just a Toy Company*

Santina had daddy issues. Her earliest memory was of a dark, frosty night. She was frantically running through the rooms in her red and green flannel pajamas, barefoot on the cool wood of the floor.

"Daddy! Daddy!"

A feeling of panic welled within her as her little feet carried her across the kitchen toward the back door where she sensed he was leaving. Her mother dashed behind her, imploring her to stop before she hurt herself.

"Daddy!" she screamed as she reached the door and pulled it open with her small hands.

A freezing gust of wind threw her back into her mother's arms. She could hear the stamping of hooves and the snorting of the enormous animals out in the darkness. She watched, shivering with cold, as the tremendous sleigh glided over the packed snow. Slowly it slid swiftly, gaining momentum, the majestic animals thundering across the frozen landscape. Suddenly, there was quiet when it lifted. A shadow sped across the ground while it rose into the blackness of the crisp night sky. They watched until the silhouette passed across the brightness of the moon. The snow glistened in the moonlight below.

"Daddy," she sniffled. Her mother rocked her trembling little body in her protective embrace.

Then she heard her father's voice echo in the night. She'd never forget it.

"Ho! Ho! Ho!" He so loved his work.

***

"Can I help you?" the school counselor asked.

She was slim and seemed rather young, not

much older than Santina. The sun pouring through the window behind her picked up the reddish highlights in her shoulder length hair. She was as disheveled as the clutter on her desk, and she glanced at it.

"So sorry. I'm a little disorganized at the moment." She frowned at her desk, mumbled something, and looked up at Santina again. "Come in. What can I do for you?"

"I'm sorry. I didn't make an appointment. I'm not really sure if you can help. My brother suggested I talk to you. It's my first year away at school, and I'm feeling..." Her voice trailed off.

She played absentmindedly with her long, white hair, and her ice-blue eyes looked at the counselor. She wore a short-sleeved pink sweater and jeans.

"Come in. Come in," the woman gestured for her to sit. "I'm new here myself." She stared for a moment. "I'm sorry. I've never seen hair that color on such a young woman. It's quite striking."

"Thanks. It's because we didn't get much sun where I grew up." Santina perched uncomfortably on the edge of the chair. "Maybe I should come back if you're busy. I can come back." Maybe this hadn't been such a good idea.

"No, no, don't be silly. Let me just clear my desk a bit." She stacked one pile on top of another. "I'm just trying to clean out this desk. I'm not sure what all these forms are for." She picked one up and squinted at it intently for a moment. "Hmm."

She looked back at Santina. "Anyway, what can I help you with?"

"Well, I'm feeling kind of overwhelmed and lost. I've never been away from home before, and everything is so different. I went to a community college, so I lived at home and now..."

"Yes, that's very common with new students. Are you having any trouble with your classes? Let me get your name." She picked up a pen.

"Oh, is this going on my record? I don't want this to jeopardize my career in the future. I don't know how all this works." Santina absentmindedly twirled her hair.

The counselor put down her pen. "How about if I don't take any notes, and we'll just talk, okay?" She paused. "Let's keep this informal. I'm Lisa."

"Okay, that sounds good. I'm Sa... Tina. I'm Tina." She relaxed back into the chair. "I love my classes. It's not about that."

"Well, then it can't be that bad." Lisa waved her hand dismissively.

Suddenly the phone on her desk rang shrilly. It startled both of them. Lisa glared at the caller ID on the display.

"Him. If he thinks he can just call whenever..." She stopped herself and cleared her throat. "Is this about a guy? Is some guy distracting you? Because sometimes they can affect your confidence." Her voice was rising. "I felt great this morning until..."

"No, it's not that," Tina interrupted quickly. "Well, unless you count my father. He..." She wasn't quite sure what to say.

"Go on," Lisa prompted.

"He was just very busy with his work. It's... uh, a business that's been in our family for generations, and it's very demanding." She stopped to gather her thoughts.

"What kind of business is it?" Lisa asked.

"It's... uh, just a toy company. It's seasonal, but he works most of the year." She paused as her emotions surfaced. "I just always felt that all the children of the world were more important than me."

This brought tears to her eyes as the pain of long-ago abandonment welled up. The sight of her father flying off had frightened her.

Lisa nodded. "I'm sure you realize that that's an

exaggeration. All the children of the world wouldn't be more important to your father than you. Now that you're grown up, you can see that he was just focused on his work." She smiled. "And, hey, it must've been fun growing up around all those toys."

Tina returned her smile. "Sometimes. I remember running through the toy shop and helping the elv... employees. They were always very nice to me."

"And what about your mother?"

Tina's face lit up. "My mother's great. She's the best. She was always there, reassuring me and baking cookies. My father loves cookies, although he's had to cut back a bit." She patted her tummy.

Lisa grinned. "She sounds wonderful. You mentioned a brother. Any other brothers or sisters?"

Tina shook her head. "I just have a younger brother. I think my father wanted a boy when I was born to carry on the family business, and then Nick was born."

"Well, then it all worked out."

"Yes, except Nick doesn't want to be involved in the business. He's a musician."

"That's too bad," Lisa said. "But let's bring this back to you. Let's talk about what's bothering you now."

"I don't know what triggered all these feelings. I guess I never felt appreciated by my father. He doesn't pay any attention to me. It's all about Nick." She thought a moment. "I don't know what anybody can do about it. I just have to deal with it."

"Do you and your brother get along?"

"Yes. Nick is just Nick. He doesn't let anything bother him," Tina answered. "I wish I could be like that."

"Have you ever tried talking to your father? He might not realize you feel this way," Lisa suggested.

"It's hard to talk to my father. He's always so distracted by work, but you're right." Tina sighed.

"What about your mother? Have you ever talked to her about how you feel?" Lisa queried.

"She just says you know how your father is. She tries to reassure me," Tina told her. "Maybe when I go home for the holidays, I can try to talk to him."

"Good," Lisa stated. "Why don't you let me know how it goes?"

"Okay." Tina stood up. She wasn't feeling very confident, but she didn't want to take up any more of Lisa's time. "I'll let you know."

***

The basement room was dark, and the music was deafening as it bounced off the walls. A young man with white, spiky hair and black eyeliner stood at the microphone, bobbing his head. He was dressed all in black, as were his fellow musicians.

"Yeaaaaaaah," he screamed into the mic. Then he held up his hand as a look of confusion crossed his face. "Hold it! Hold it!" he yelled above the screeching guitar and pounding drums. "What's the lyric here?" He pointed to a sheet on the music stand before him. "Is it 'death in my heart' or 'death in my head'?" He stared at it. "Man, who wrote this? It's illegible."

"You did, Nick," answered the bass guitarist. "I think you said it was 'death in your head' because the bureaucracy has stifled your creativity."

"Yeah, that's right." Nick nodded. "That's exactly what happened. I'm stifled. That's exactly right." He stared at the paper, mouthing some words. "Hold it. What's that sound? It sounds like a bell. Good sound effect. I like it. Who's on it?"

"I think it's your phone, man," said the drummer. He pushed his dreadlocks from his face and grabbed his water bottle. "It's hot in here. I'm taking a break."

"Okay, cool. Take five, everyone," Nick called out. He pulled his cell phone from his pocket. "Who the hell is interrupting our rehearsal?" He looked at the phone and then put it to his ear. "Tina? What's up?"

"Hi Nick," Tina said into the mouthpiece for her earbuds while she held her phone.

She was strolling outside in the sunny courtyard on the school campus. There was a large, circular fountain that students milled around or sat on the edge talking or eating lunch. "Can you hear me?"

"Yeah. You're totally audible. How's school?" Nick asked her.

"It's fine."

"I don't know how you can subject yourself to that kind of brainwashing. It's mind control."

Tina rolled her eyes. He was always going on about crazy stuff. "How's the band doing?"

"Stellar. We've got a gig coming up, so we've been rehearsing and I wrote some new songs," he told her. "One's called 'Frost in My Head' and the other is called 'Black Snow.'"

"I can't wait to hear them."

"It's great," he enthused. "I'm really getting in touch with my inner darkness."

"That's good," she humored him. "I was wondering when you're going home for the holidays."

"Don't know if I can. We've got this gig coming up."

"Nick! You have to! We always have the holidays together, and you know I can't deal with Mom and Dad alone. At least not Dad."

"I know. It's intense," he acknowledged. "Don't let Dad freak you. He's just obsessed with work. Let it roll off."

"You make it sound easy," she said. "I'll try, but please promise me you'll think about coming home."

"I might make it for Thanksgiving, but I'm over the holiday thing. I'm not into commercial, materialistic gratification. We're not little kids anymore, and I'm past it. I don't even want to acknowledge it. You know, the whole judgment thing. Naughty or nice. It's repressive. I mean, I should write a song about it. The repression of expression. Kids can't be free to be themselves because they'll be judged. Let kids be kids, man! Let kids be free!"

Tina sighed. "Okay, Nick. Hope the gig is great."

"Thanks. I've got to find some paper."

"Okay. Talk soon."

"I can't find a pen."

Tina sat down on the edge of the fountain and watched the water cascade down into the pool below. The sun's reflection rippled on the surface from the gentle breeze that played with her long, straight white hair.

She wished she could be more like Nick. He was following his dreams and never worried about anyone's expectations.

***

Clara had short, white hair and wore green, baggy pants and a red tank top. She looked at the TV and slowly breathed in and out before attempting the Downward Dog pose that was being demonstrated. She was more flexible from when she'd begun doing yoga, and she was pleased that the Tree pose had improved her balance. This was important as she aged. She was determined that she and her husband stay healthy. Her yoga routine ended with the Child's pose. It was her favorite because it stretched out her lower back and felt good as she relaxed into it.

Ding! The timer went off in the kitchen. She pulled herself up and went to check on the scones. They were lightly browned and looked perfect. She took them from the oven and placed the cookie sheet on a cooling rack, leaning over to savor the aroma.

"Mmm."

She turned to the blender to finish making her smoothie, adding a scoop of super green powder to the almond milk and banana and switched it on. Then she returned to the TV with a smoothie in hand and a green mustache adorning her upper lip.

"Yum."

Clara removed the DVD and turned off the TV. She pulled a red and green flannel shirt over her tank top before settling on the floor into the Lotus pose. With legs crossed and eyes closed, she waited for the scones to cool.

***

"Walter, how long have we worked together?" Santa asked.

He leaned back in his chair behind the big mahogany desk. His white hair was tousled, and he stroked his long, white beard and mustache. His red and green checked flannel shirt matched Clara's, and he wore baggy jeans.

"Drat! I wish I could shave. This beard drives me crazy sometimes." He leaned forward. "The point is, we're heading for a crisis. You've been with me a long time, Walter. We've always worked well together, but Clara is talking about retiring, and Nick isn't ready to take over. He's still going through that stupid music phase. It'd be unheard of to go outside the family. This business has been in my family, well, since the beginning."

Walter nodded patiently. He'd heard it all before. He was seated in a chair on the opposite side of the desk. His short elf legs dangled above the floor. His dark hair matched his solemn eyes. He knew Santa well enough to let him vent while he simply nodded silently. Every few months, he talked about retiring, but Walter knew Santa loved it too much to retire, despite his frequent grumbling and complaining.

Santa looked over at the framed family photos on his desk and on the bookshelves. The children were so cute when they were little. Where had he failed?

"I always hoped Nick would come around," he said sadly. "What will happen to all the children if I retire? No presents?" He raised his voice. "No Christmas? I'll never let that happen."

Walter nodded again. "Why don't you ask Nick again this year? Maybe he's realized that a music career is harder than he thought and he's gotten it out of his system. Maybe he's matured enough to realize..."

Santa waved his hand. "I always assumed I'd pass the business on to my son. Generations of men in my family have passed it on and kept it going. It's tradition. It's an honor. It's part of being a Claus. I never thought twice about it. It's not too much to ask, is it?"

Walter bobbed his head. "I know." He wondered if the time was right. "I hate to bring this up but, as the foreman, we do need to discuss a few things."

"What?" Santa exclaimed. "I thought the union was happy with our last contract."

"Yes, we are. There are just a few things." He put his thumb and index finger close together. "Not much, really. I've hired more elves as we agreed, but I hired bigger elves in order..."

"Bigger elves?" Santa bellowed. "What are you talking about?"

"I have a few bigger elves starting orientation today. You know, like your size. I think it's good to have some diversity, and the bigger elves have a distinct set of skills from our other elves. It's practical, and the union is behind it," Walter explained.

"The union," Santa repeated with disdain. "What else? Just keep ruining my mood, Walter."

"Well, the United North Pole Workers have been interested in updating things for a while, as you know."

"You're talking about automating the line again, aren't you?" Santa accused. "You know how I feel about that. Everything must be made by hand. I know it's more work, but quality is the most important thing. We can't cut corners."

"Yes, I agree," Walter acknowledged. "Quality is essential, but every year we have more and more children to make toys for, and it's getting increasingly difficult to keep up. If we could just automate some steps, it would really..."

"Out of the question!" Santa said emphatically. "We've been doing it this way for generations and I will not compromise the quality of the toys. Hire more elves if you must."

"I did. They're starting today," Walter said evenly. "But, eventually, we're going to run out of room, and I don't see how we can keep up with demand..."

"Don't be so negative," Santa replied. "So, we have a few million more kids every year. What's the problem?

May your life be filled with great books!

Made in the USA
Las Vegas, NV
15 January 2022

41491755R00139